PEOPLE
IN THE NEWS

Tony Blair

by Corinne J. Naden and Rose Blue

LUCENT BOOKS®

THOMSON
GALE

San Diego • Detroit • New York • San Francisco • Cleveland
New Haven, Conn. • Waterville, Maine • London • Munich

THOMSON

✳

™

GALE

Titles in the People in the News series include:

Tim Allen
Drew Barrymore
Tony Blair
Garth Brooks
George W. Bush
Jim Carrey
Michael Crichton
Matt Damon
Celine Dion
Michael J. Fox
Bill Gates
Mel Gibson
John Grisham
Jesse Jackson
Michael Jackson
Michael Jordan
Stephen King

George Lucas
Madonna
Rosie O'Donnell
Brad Pitt
Colin Powell
Princess Diana
Prince William
Christopher Reeve
Julia Roberts
The Rolling Stones
J.K. Rowling
Steven Spielberg
R.L. Stine
Sting
John Travolta
Oprah Winfrey
Tiger Woods

For more information, contact
Lucent Books
27500 Drake Rd.
Farmington Hills, MI 48331-3535
Or you can visit our Internet site at http://www.gale.com

LIBRARY OF CONGRESS CATALOGING-IN-PUBLICATION DATA

Naden, Corinne J.
   Tony Blair / by Corinne J. Naden and Rose Blue.
      p. cm. —— (People in the news)
   Summary: Profiles the childhood, education, politics, election, and possible future of the British prime minister Tony Blair.
   Includes bibliographical references and index.
      ISBN 1-59018-236-7 (alk. paper)
   1. Blair, Tony, 1953–   Juvenile literature. 2. Prime ministers—Great Britain——Biography——Juvenile literature. [1. Blair, Tony, 1953– 2. Prime ministers.] I. Blue, Rose. II. Title. III. People in the news (San Diego, Calif.)
   DA591.B56 N33 2003
   941.085'092——dc21

                                                              2002007174

Table of Contents

Foreword

FAME AND CELEBRITY are alluring. People are drawn to those who walk in fame's spotlight, whether they are known for great accomplishments or for notorious deeds. The lives of the famous pique public interest and attract attention, perhaps because their experiences seem in some ways so different from, yet in other ways so similar to, our own.

Newspapers, magazines, and television regularly capitalize on this fascination with celebrity by running profiles of famous people. For example, television programs such as *Entertainment Tonight* devote all of their programming to stories about entertainment and entertainers. Magazines such as *People* fill their pages with stories of the private lives of famous people. Even newspapers, newsmagazines, and television news frequently delve into the lives of well-known personalities. Despite the number of articles and programs, few provide more than a superficial glimpse at their subjects.

Lucent's People in the News series offers young readers a deeper look into the lives of today's newsmakers, the influences that have shaped them, and the impact they have had in their fields of endeavor and on other people's lives. The subjects of the series hail from many disciplines and walks of life. They include authors, musicians, athletes, political leaders, entertainers, entrepreneurs, and others who have made a mark on modern life and who, in many cases, will continue to do so for years to come.

These biographies are more than factual chronicles. Each book emphasizes the contributions, accomplishments, or deeds that have brought fame or notoriety to the individual and shows how that person has influenced modern life. Authors portray their subjects in a realistic, unsentimental light. For example, Bill Gates—the cofounder and chief executive officer of the software giant Microsoft—has been instrumental in making personal computers the most vital tool of the modern age. Few dispute his business savvy, his perseverance, or his technical expertise, yet critics say he is ruthless in his dealings with competitors and driven more by his desire to maintain Microsoft's dominance in the computer industry than by an interest in furthering technology.

In these books, young readers will encounter inspiring stories about real people who achieved success despite enormous obstacles. Oprah Winfrey—the most powerful, most watched, and wealthiest woman on television today—spent the first six years of her life in the care of her grandparents while her unwed mother sought work and a better life elsewhere. Her adolescence was colored by promiscuity, pregnancy at age fourteen, rape, and sexual abuse.

Each author documents and supports his or her work with an array of primary and secondary source quotations taken from diaries, letters, speeches, and interviews. All quotes are footnoted to show readers exactly how and where biographers derive their information and provide guidance for further research. The quotations enliven the text by giving readers eyewitness views of the life and accomplishments of each person covered in the People in the News series.

In addition, each book in the series includes photographs, annotated bibliographies, timelines, and comprehensive indexes. For both the casual reader and the student researcher, the People in the News series offers insight into the lives of today's newsmakers—people who shape the way we live, work, and play in the modern age.

Introduction

England Gets a New Look

Ever since he was elected prime minister in 1997, Great Britain's charismatic Tony Blair has been trying to modernize his generally conservative nation. Blair is head of the Labour Party, although he is unlike any of its previous leaders. He is too young to have experienced most of Labour's long struggle against the Conservative Party in Great Britain; in fact, he is the youngest prime minister in nearly two hundred years.

The British people show a willingness to listen to Tony Blair, and most are pleased with many of the changes he has made since he was elected to office. But when he wants to make profound changes in the way Great Britain operates, such as becoming more closely tied to other European nations, the country is not so sure.

Tony Blair has become an international player since being elected prime minister. When Yugoslavia became embroiled in a bitter struggle in 1999, Blair called for sending British troops into Kosovo. When the United States was attacked by terrorists on September 11, 2001, Blair was the first U.S. ally to offer not only assistance but his own presence. Within days of the attack, he flew to the United States to demonstrate Britain's aid and encouragement. Blair has become America's biggest supporter.

Most people like Tony Blair. He is charming, handsome, energetic, friendly, and forceful. Whether laughing or crying, he appears sincere, and he seems passionate about what he believes will make his country a better and stronger place.

Tony Blair is the youngest prime minister Great Britain has had in nearly two hundred years.

But Blair has his critics, too. They say his charm masks a determined, even ruthless politician. Indeed, there have been instances before and after his becoming prime minister that reveal this determination. Critics question whether a real statesman exists behind the charisma and wonder if Blair is merely a clever politician.

Tony Blair won a second term as prime minister in 2001 after an election with very little turnout from the public. Though most think that, overall, Blair has been a competent prime minister, he still faces a number of challenges. Blair says he is a man with a vision. He sees himself as a strong leader, one who will lead his country down a new path. His critics, however, claim that he has not clearly explained what that new path entails. Many people have also not been convinced of Blair's progress in handling domestic problems, especially those regarding education, the public transportation system, and the administration of health care. Blair now has to prove himself to both his admirers and his critics.

Chapter 1

From Scotland to London

Tony Blair was born in Edinburgh, Scotland, at the Queen Mary Maternity Home on May 6, 1953. His father, Leo, was a lawyer who ran for Parliament as a member of the Conservative Party, also called the Tories. His mother, Hazel, was the daughter of a Glasgow butcher. Since her husband was away from home much of the time, she was the one who taught their three children loyalty, duty, and a sense of social conscience, values that would shape Blair as a man, politician, husband, and father.

Tony, the middle child, was named Anthony Charles Lynton Blair. Tony never knew the origin of his middle names until he was an adult. Leo Blair had been adopted, and his natural parents were actors and dancers. Leo's father was Charles Parsons, whose stage name was Jimmy Lynton. Although Tony knew about his father's adoption, Leo never spoke of his natural parents. So when Tony was campaigning for office and the *Daily Mail* ran their names, he was quite surprised to learn that he had been named after his natural grandfather.

Leo's early years were difficult; his foster parents provided him with a good home but they had very little money. So, Leo quit school at age seventeen to go to work. Then, World War II broke out and he joined the army. He entered as a private and left as a major. Upon discharge, he married and earned a law degree. He was offered a job halfway around the world at the University of Adelaide, Australia, where he lectured in administrative law. For three years, the Blair family lived in Adelaide, where Tony's sister, Sarah, was born. They returned in 1958,

Durham Cathedral (above) is where Chorister School is found, the school Tony Blair attended.

and Leo Blair became a lecturer at Durham, one of England's major universities.

At the time of Tony's birth, his father had been a junior tax inspector studying for a law degree at night. (In fact, all three Blair children grew up to be lawyers.) Leo Blair was a determined person, and he passed on that determination to Tony. Ambitious and self-made, Leo was adamant that his children receive the best education. So, William (Tony's older brother) and Tony were sent to the Chorister School, which is part of the nine-hundred-year-old cathedral at Durham.

An Emerging Personality

Blair Two, as Tony was known, loved the Chorister, and apparently the school brought out the best in his personality. According to one of the masters, "The thing everyone who taught Blair remembers about him was his smile. He had an almost impish smile; it could light up a room."[1] Outgoing and dramatic, he was an all-around model schoolboy. Tony was a good student, played cricket and rugby, acted in school plays, and sang in the choir. He was not, however, politically involved, except for becoming the school's Conservative candidate in a mock election when he was twelve. But he was given that role because his father was a rather well-known Conservative by that time, not because of any of Tony's convictions.

During those early school years, Tony Blair does not remember seeing much of his father. An extroverted, entertaining public speaker, Leo was in great demand. Besides his law duties, his work as chairman of the Durham Conservative Association kept him away from home a good deal. Then, in 1963, he decided to run for Parliament as a Tory, and Tony learned later that his father had ambitions of becoming prime minister. But just before the election, Leo's world—and that of the entire Blair family —came tumbling down.

Trouble for the Blairs

Leo Blair suffered a massive stroke in 1964, which had a devastating effect on all of the family. At first, the doctors were not sure he would live. And for a long time it seemed that he might never speak again. For three years, Leo did not utter a word. Tony, who was ten years old, and his brother and sister were deeply shocked. He said later, "You think as a child your parents are indestructible; that they will live for ever. But there was my father, unable to speak, having been lucky to survive."[2] Blair also said that the day his father had a stroke was "the day my childhood ended."[3] Of his mother, Tony remembered that she "was an absolute rock. I didn't see her break down, never once, . . . she must have been under awful strain. But she never exhibited any signs of it, so I owe her a very great debt."[4]

For the next three years, young Tony and his mother were responsible for the household, since William was attending a boarding school outside of Edinburgh. As his father was getting better, tragedy struck again: Tony's sister developed a form of juvenile rheumatoid arthritis known as Still's disease, which wears away the cartilage that protects bones and in time wears out a person's joints. Sarah was in the hospital for two years. Caring for both his sister and his father imposed discipline on the young boy. Although Leo's health gradually improved, all of his lost ambitions now shifted to his children, and Tony did not want to disappoint him. "I felt I couldn't let him down,"[5] he said. Already disposed to succeed in whatever he did, Tony became even more driven than before.

On to Public School

When Tony reached the age of thirteen, he was sent away to public school (in Great Britain, private schools that charge tuition are generally known as public schools). The second Blair son followed his brother to the well-respected Fettes College on the outskirts of Edinburgh. One of the best known public schools in Scotland, Fettes, founded in 1870, was old-fashioned and very rigid.

Blair began boarding at Fettes in 1966 after winning an "exhibition," or scholarship. Unlike at his previous school, Blair was miserable at Fettes, especially during the first year. Part of it had to do with the rigid system of discipline that required junior boys to become, in effect, servants to senior boys. The juniors did such things as shine shoes and lay out clothes. At the time, seniors were also allowed to beat the younger boys with a cane if a senior decided that, for example, his shoes did not have the proper shine. Blair was beaten on a number of occasions for infractions. He was a junior servant to Michael Gascoigne, now a lawyer. Apparently, Blair never forgot the experience. Years later, in 1990, when he was the guest speaker at a lawyers' club in Edinburgh, he saw Gascoigne in the audience and could not resist noting in his speech that his evening had been ruined.

Blair's unhappiness at Fettes set him on a collision course with authority, both at school and at home. He started to rebel against his father. On a couple of occasions when he was supposed to be taking a train home for a visit, he rode past his station with the vague idea of running away. But each time, he changed his mind and returned home. Blair later remembered that painful period: "At school I was somewhat rebellious. . . .

007 Goes to Fettes

Suspense-fiction novelist Ian Fleming thought so much of Fettes College that he bestowed its diploma upon one of the twentieth century's most popular fiction heroes. Fleming wrote twelve novels of international espionage and intrigue starring the high-living and stylish British secret agent 007, also known as James Bond. He gave Bond a Fettes education and sent him off into a world of daring escapes, violent action, gambling, and fast cars. The handsome, debonair Bond became everyone's superhero, and the books, several made into motion pictures, sold more than 18 million copies.

Pierce Brosnan plays James Bond in the movie Tomorrow Never Dies.

I was never an out-and-out rebel, but I was a rationalist in the sense that, if certain things went wrong, I would say so."[6]

However, one bright spot at Fettes for Blair was headmaster Eric Anderson. Anderson set up a new house at Fettes called Arniston, which Blair joined during his second year. It was a far more liberal place in which some of the old rules were thrown out. For instance, there were no beatings at Arniston, nor did anyone act as a servant to the seniors. The highest priority became academic excellence. For Blair, it was a welcome change, and he actually began to enjoy some of his time spent at Fettes. Blair always retained the highest respect for the headmaster, and Anderson, in turn, remembered his young charge with fondness.

During his years at Fettes, Blair is probably best remembered as an actor. Encouraged by Anderson, he began to take part in the school drama productions. At fifteen years old, he won the part of Mark Antony in the school production of *Julius Caesar.* The school magazine, the *Fettesian,* found him youthful but certainly promising. The next year, Blair and five other boys formed an acting group called the Pseuds that presented contemporary works such as Harold Pinter's *The Dumb Waiter.* Blair's greatest dramatic success at Fettes came in 1971 when he was Captain Stanhope in R.C. Sherriff's *Journey's End,* a play set in the trenches of World War I.

Besides drama, Blair developed another interest at Fettes—girls. To this day, he has remained close friends with two of the girls he met at that time. One was Anji Hunter, whom he met at a friend's home in 1970. The daughter of a rubber plantation boss who lived in Malaysia until she was ten, Hunter was even more disdainful of authority than Blair was. She constantly questioned the system and was expelled for insubordination from St. Leonard's, the Fettes sister school. The two met again at Oxford during Blair's first year there. Although they were never romantically involved, they did become close friends. When Blair was elected prime minister, Hunter, who was by then married with two children, became one of the small group of trusted people who advised him on political affairs.

Blair's first girlfriend, Amanda Mackenzie Stuart, was also the first girl admitted to Fettes. They, too, remained close friends into adulthood, and each went to the other's wedding. Stuart remembers that Blair was "not really into politics at the time—it was more [the rock bands] Led Zeppelin and Cream—but I was never surprised that he joined [the] Labour [Party]. That was always there."[7]

Despite his early misery at Fettes and his disdain of its rigid system, Blair readily agrees that, without his education, he would never have become prime minister. It gave him not only the academic background he needed but also the confidence and style that would carry him successfully, if not always smoothly, into the tumultuous world of politics.

Filling in a Gap

At eighteen years old, Blair left Fettes, not for Oxford or another university but for a nonacademic year that filled in the gap between classrooms. One of Blair's friends later said, "He should be embarrassed about that year. That was before he became respectable."[8]

It is doubtful that the future prime minister was embarrassed at all. He was too busy having a good time. He spent most of the year in London arranging work for small bands, mostly young men who were caught up in the growing rock frenzy and

Mick Jagger, the Knight

In June 2002, Blair nominated Mick Jagger, longtime leader of the rock band the Rolling Stones, for knighthood. When a person is knighted, he or she receives the Most Excellent Order of the British Empire. Since 1917, the British monarch has given this honor for outstanding service to the nation or outstanding achievement in a particular field. It confers upon the recipient the title of sir or dame. In nominating Jagger, the prime minister praised his years of contributions to rock music and his genius as a musician. The British press also suggested that Blair's long admiration for Jagger and his music was a factor in the nomination.

One of the most popular and long-lived of all rock bands, the Rolling Stones are known for biting lyrics and expressive instrumental accompaniments. The band hit its popularity in the late 1960s and early 1970s with such albums as *Beggar's Banquet* and *Let It Bleed*. Long after the Beatles and other famous rock groups have disbanded, the Rolling Stones play on.

Mick Jagger (center) was nominated by Blair for knighthood in 2002.

dreamed of becoming stars. Blair himself loved the Rolling Stones; he imitated lead singer Mick Jagger by wearing his hair below his shoulders and often sporting a large brown fur coat.

The gigs that Blair arranged were small, holding an audience of about 150. But Blair loved organizing parties so much that, with his friend Alan Collenette, he decided to celebrate his nineteenth birthday on May 6, 1972, with a big bash. He and Collenette staged a live concert in Queen Alexandria Hall in Kensington featuring a number of rock bands. The hall could hold two thousand people, but practically no one came. This incident may have prompted Blair to think about a more stable career and returning to school.

Oddly enough, when considering his future career, Tony Blair showed no interest in politics. Most statesmen point with pride to their early political leanings or their admiration for a political figure, but not Blair. He chose law instead.

A Lad at Oxford

Blair returned to his studies, this time at Oxford University, in the autumn of 1972. Located northwest of London, Oxford is the nation's oldest university; its University College was founded in 1249. It is also one of the world's most prestigious centers of higher learning.

Although it was not his intention, Blair had chosen the perfect school for a future politician. The Oxford name carries great prestige and is home to two noted student newspapers, the *Cherwell* and *Isis,* in which students can write about political philosophy and may even get noticed by the students' groups, the Oxford Union and the Oxford Labour Party. However, Blair never joined the Labour Party at Oxford, or any group of particular note. He never wrote for either of the student newspapers, and he went to the Oxford Union just once. Looking back, Blair remembers Oxford in this way:

> I think, like all big institutions, far from being intellectually invigorating, it is actually rather stifling. There was very little room for fresh or original thought. . . . So when I look back at my time at Oxford I have extremely fond

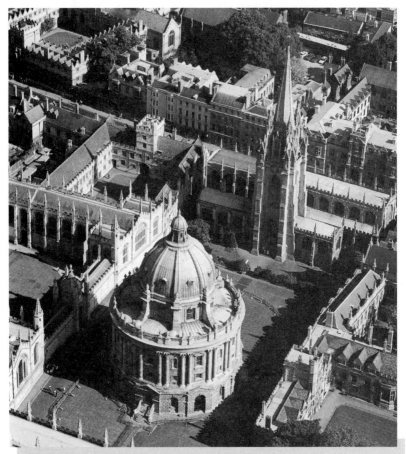

Blair attended Oxford University, a school known for its prestigious reputation.

memories of the friends I made there, but all the time I was at Oxford I felt like an outsider.[9]

On the social scene, however, Blair was no outsider. In addition to his studies, Blair managed a full social life at St. John's College in Oxford. He joined the Archery Club, which despite its name was dedicated more to staging elaborate dinners than to shooting bows and arrows. He also played in a rock band called the Ugly Rumours. As lead singer, he would never be confused with Mick Jagger, but he would walk out on the stage with long hair and a shirt unbuttoned to the waist, punching the air. The audiences loved it. He might have been out of his element at Oxford but not on the stage.

One might think that Blair had little time for study while he was enjoying himself at the university. In fact, he applied himself as diligently as he needed to and worked very hard in some of his law courses. Blair had decided to walk in his father's and older brother's footsteps and become a lawyer. Since then, he has said on more than one occasion that he wished he had studied history instead.

The Intellectual Group

It was not law or history, however, but religion that became a stimulating subject to Blair at Oxford. Long after he graduated,

The interior of Westminster Cathedral. Blair was confirmed in the Church of England.

Blair said that he started to become serious about his religious feelings and his political ones at the same time. This came about through his association with an intense group of undergraduate students from overseas. One student was Peter Thomson, a thirty-six-year-old minister of the Australian Anglican church, who described himself as a renegade priest. Blair calls him "the person who most influenced me."[10] He met Thomson through Geoff Gallop, a Rhodes scholar and a declared revolutionary Marxist (a person who follows the ideas of Marxism, a form of political thought in which both private property and the distribution of income are controlled by society rather than by individuals). Also in the group were Marc Palley from Rhodesia, an atheist who became Blair's best friend, and Olara Otunno, a Christian from Uganda who would later be the Ugandan foreign minister.

Through long and what Blair remembers as spellbinding conversations with the diverse group, he gradually developed his own religious and political convictions. Today, Blair is a practicing Christian and lives his faith on a day-to-day basis. He was confirmed in the Church of England near the end of his second year at Oxford.

Although Blair keeps his religious beliefs private, he regards the teachings of Christianity as important to his political views. For Blair, his commitment to religion began to develop into a serious sense of wanting to do something, to make a difference. In time, this would lead to an interest in politics.

Despite Blair's newfound interest in things political and his voracious reading of various liberal texts, he still did not become politically active while at Oxford. He did, however, join a sit-in with two thousand other students in support of a central student union. He also became involved in a campaign against apartheid in South Africa, which institutionalized racial discrimination against its black citizens.

The group broke up at the end of Blair's second year, the summer of 1974. Blair kept in touch with them, however. In fact, Thomson went to London when Blair became prime minister.

During his final year at Oxford, Blair and Palley shared a house with three female undergraduates. Blair graduated in June

1975 with a second-place ranking in the Oxford grading system, rather than the top first.

Blair returned home an Oxford graduate with left-wing political leanings (meaning he was generally against big business and for workers' rights) and with law school waiting in the fall. Two weeks after his return, however, his mother died. Hazel Blair was fifty-one years old and had been diagnosed with cancer while Tony was still at Fettes. Although he knew of her illness, Blair blamed himself for never realizing how serious it was. Actually, his mother and father had not told him about her worsening health for fear that he would do poorly on his final exams.

Blair's mother's death was devastating to him. She had been the glue that held the family together through his father's stroke and his sister's illness. Blair adored his mother and she him. Even though he had never been as close to his father, he was especially kind to him during this period. Later, Blair said that his mother's death made him grow up and start to take a more serious view of life in general.

Off to London

Three months after his mother's death, in September 1975, Blair began his one-year course at bar (law) school. He and Palley moved into a basement flat, or apartment, in west London. As law school progressed, Blair realized that he had chosen to study law because he did not know what else to study, not because of any real passion for it. Now he began to see law as a base for a career in politics, which genuinely interested him. He decided to become a member of Britain's Labour Party.

Labour is one of the two major political parties in Great Britain. Traditionally, the Labour Party is concerned with issues of social welfare and workers' rights, nationalization of industries, and full employment. Its opposition is the Conservative Party, or Tories. The Conservatives are generally the party of free enterprise, private ownership, and law and order, and have a reluctance to get involved monetarily in a European union. Blair's natural inclination to go against the established order, plus his growing belief that Labour offered British workers a better future, drew him to the party.

A person joining the Labour Party was technically supposed to be a member of a trade union. Blair was not. However, the Labour group in Blair's Chelsea district had long been inactive and disorganized. So, when Blair and a few others asked to join, the rules were relaxed in order to bring new vitality into the group. To fulfill the Labour Party's requirement, Blair later became a member of the Transport and General Workers Union.

Once Blair joined the party, he became very enthusiastic about bringing Labour's message to the British public. As a result of his enthusiasm, he soon became the secretary of the Chelsea district group. His duties were mainly delivering pamphlets and attending meetings, which Blair did for about a year. He changed during this period from the cheerful, fun-filled lad of his school days to a more serious and thoughtful young man. He kept up his law studies, carried out his secretarial duties, and, according to Palley, frequently read the Bible at night.

As Blair became more involved in politics, he became aware that the Labour Party in general was not operating as a smooth political machine. Despite the fact that Labour leader Harold Wilson had won his fourth general election as prime minister, Blair thought that the leadership seemed to rely mainly on the unions to stay in power. Unions often directed their members to vote for certain candidates, which meant that Labour could generally depend on huge blocks of votes. But Blair felt that Labour was now out of step with the real feelings and concerns of the regular people who made up the party. In Blair's eyes, Labour needed a boost.

Passing the Bar

As concerned as he was, Blair was not yet in a position to change party politics. His first priority was to find work. In the spring of 1976, he applied for a scholarship. In order to practice law in England, students studying for the bar exam must go to work— for the experience, not money—with a group of lawyers who share offices. An institution known as the Inns of Court offered some scholarships for this no-pay period, and in the spring of 1976, Blair applied. On application day, the applicants were seated in alphabetical order. Next to Blair was a woman named Cherie Booth; she would eventually become Tony Blair's wife.

Cherie Booth Blair

Raised in a working-class Liverpool family, Cherie Booth has become one of London's most respected lawyers. She was born in Lancashire on September 23, 1954, to actors Gale Smith and Tony Booth. Her father gained fame on the British TV series *Till Death Us Do Part,* which inspired the well-known American sitcom *All in the Family.* When Cherie was seven, her father left the family, which then included her younger sister Lyndsey. Her mother supported them by working in a fish-and-chip shop. Despite her father's desertion, when he was badly burned in an accident in 1979, Cherie helped him to recover from many operations.

Like Tony Blair, Cherie had a taste for the theater at an early age. At first, she wanted to be a ballerina, a career that she jokingly said was shortened by the fact that she has no sense of balance. She became a member of the Labour Party Youth at age sixteen and often said that she wanted to become the nation's first female prime minister.

Booth was one of the most gifted of that year's law students and achieved the highest first in law at the London School of Economics. She also got a scholarship. Blair did not.

Booth and Blair met again as pupils under a lawyer named Derry Irvine. Booth had already been accepted when Blair applied. Although Irvine had not planned on taking on another pupil, he accepted Blair because he was impressed with the young man's enthusiasm.

In the summer of 1976, Blair and Booth took the bar exams. She scored an impressive first, he a rather unimpressive third. Later, Blair said, "I didn't work particularly hard at it."[11] After the exams, Booth went to work and Blair went to France, where he earned money tending bar for the summer.

When Blair returned to London, he and Booth began work as friendly professionals. But soon they began to date and the relationship changed to romance. After dating for about two years, Blair proposed in 1979. Tony and Cherie married in the chapel of St. John's College, Oxford, on March 29, 1980. Blair's brother, William, was his best man. Besides the wedding itself, Blair remembers that, as a promise to his new wife, he gave up smoking on that day, having his last cigarette fifteen minutes before the ceremony.

Blair pictured with his wife, Cherie. Cherie has become one of London's most respected attorneys.

Blair was now nearly twenty-seven years old and newly married with a promising law practice before him. But he was increasingly becoming involved in the politics of the Labour Party. This involvement would soon overshadow his work as a lawyer and become his full-time career.

Chapter 2

Changing
the Old Guard

Tony Blair's rise from a new member in a small Chelsea district to head of the Labour Party of Great Britain in just fourteen years was remarkable, and many factors contributed to his success. Already charismatic, Blair became a well-spoken politician with a knack for making his audience believe what he was saying. He worked hard at whatever job he was given in the party. He became adept at sizing up a problem quickly and getting right to the heart of the matter. This was important in moving swiftly up the party ranks. After making some initial mistakes, Blair learned when to speak out on issues and when to be silent. And he learned to stay in the good graces of those already in power.

First Tries

Blair's involvement in politics started in earnest when he and Cherie, after a honeymoon in France, moved to a home in Hackney. They became members of the Queensbridge branch of the Hackney South Labour Party in late 1980. Blair had already taken a baby step in party politics by writing some articles for the left-wing magazine *New Statesman,* in which he articulated his views on such matters as employment laws and the right to strike.

After spending most of his life ignoring politics, Blair now lost no time getting involved. One month after he and his wife attended their first meeting at Hackney, Blair decided to stand for a seat in Parliament. (Americans "run" for a seat in Congress; the English "stand" for Parliament.) In December 1980, he became one of seventeen party members vying to be Labour's candidate from Middlesbrough, near Blair's boyhood home in Durham. To become a candidate, a person had to be nominated by either a local union or a branch of the party. Blair got the vote of the electricians' union, but none of the other unions supported him. The seat was won by Stuart Bell.

The next Blair attempt for Parliament came in the fall of 1981, but this time it was not Tony but Cherie who tried. She lost her bid for a seat in a by-election, which is an election held in an off year in order to fill a vacancy. Some of their friends thought that had she won that election, she might have been the Blair in the family to eventually become prime minister. But after that loss, Booth (who retained her name professionally) returned permanently to law and, as noted in *Current Leaders of Nations,* went on to become "one of London's most successful and best known lawyers."[12]

In 1982, Tony Blair again decided to stand for Parliament. This time, he stood for a seat from Beaconsfield. Since this was

Blair stood for a seat in Britain's Parliament three times before winning. The House of Parliament (below) is where Parliament meets.

Margaret Thatcher, the Iron Lady

In 1979, Margaret Thatcher became the United Kingdom's first female prime minister when the Conservatives finally overcame the party's loss of the previous two general elections. Thatcher was seen as a decisive new voice of the Conservatives. She called for greater individual freedom and an end to excessive government interference in the economy. In later years, her policies and dominance of party leaders earned her the title of "Iron Lady."

Thatcher, born in Lincolnshire in 1925, was the daughter of a grocer. At Oxford University, she became the first female president of the Oxford University Conservative Association. Her first stand for Parliament in 1950 was unsuccessful, but she was elected nine years later. She succeeded Prime Minister Edward Heath as leader of the Conservatives in 1975. A split in the Conservative ranks over politics regarding the European Union led to her resignation in late 1990.

generally considered a safe district for the Conservatives, not many Labour candidates applied. But Blair thought it was worth a try nonetheless. Tony Blair received the Labour nomination to stand against the Conservatives for the Beaconsfield seat on April 1, 1982. On April 2, the Falkland Islands were invaded by Argentina. Blair lost the Beaconsfield seat, many observers say, because of his controversial remarks on the Falklands during his campaign.

Blair and the Falkland Islands

The Falklands, about three hundred miles to the northeast off the southern tip of South America, had long been the subject of dispute between Argentina and the United Kingdom. Since the early twentieth century, Argentina had claimed it owned the islands, but Great Britain had claimed ownership since 1833. The matter was even brought before the United Nations in 1964. Rather than make a ruling, the UN essentially told the two countries to settle the problem themselves. Little was heard about the Falklands until 1982 when Argentina began to make public claims of ownership once again and then invaded the islands. The war lasted two months, until a British naval task force steamed into the area and took the territory.

The Falkland incident was a boost for Britain's Conservative Party and a setback for Labour. Conservative popularity had been fading because of a rise in unemployment, but it soared when Prime Minister Margaret Thatcher took a firm stand on sending a task force against Argentina. In fact, Thatcher became so popular that the Conservatives would win a landslide victory in the general election the following year. Labour, however, suffered both from Thatcher's popularity and from its less decisive stand on the issue.

Blair's speeches on the Falklands illustrated his campaigning problem. He called for sending a task force to the Falklands, but he seemed to sit on both sides of the issue when he said, "At the same time I want a negotiated settlement and I believe that given the starkness of the military options we need to compromise on certain things. I don't think that ultimately the wishes of the Falkland islanders must determine our position."[13] Thatcher had said exactly the opposite. She declared that what Falkland

Margaret Thatcher was Britain's first female prime minister.

citizens wanted was indeed the determining factor, and the British public approved. In addition, some of the media thought that Blair's remarks were rough. He sounded as though he believed that someone who illegally takes something should be allowed to keep it in order to avoid a fight.

The Falkland Islands incident taught Blair important things about political campaigning, such as sounding decisive while speaking about an issue. It also taught him the importance of being clearly understood. He learned to look at an issue from all sides before giving an opinion. Blair lost his campaign for the Beaconsfield seat, but his defeat did teach him some politi-

Marines await a helicopter bound for the Falkland Islands. The Falkland Islands became a campaign issue for Blair in 1982.

cal lessons that he never forgot. However, with Labour dropping from second to third place behind another political party, the Liberals, it was a disappointing first race for the future prime minister.

Out of his first loss, Blair did experience one positive outcome. His campaign style brought him recognition by most of the important Labour leaders. They found him to be charming, attractive, entertaining, and, despite his remarks on the Falklands, well informed. They liked what he stood for. As Blair spoke out on more and more issues, he defined himself as being in support of abortion rights, gay rights, and racial equality and against the death penalty. He also advocated more involvement by Great Britain in European affairs. Blair was developing his own political philosophy that would one day lead the Labour Party.

General Election Time

Blair got over the disappointment of losing the bid for the Beaconsfield seat by going back to work and preparing for future elections. It looked as though the next general election would be called the following year, in 1983. General elections in Britain do not operate on a specific-term basis, as they do every four years in the United States. The party in power in Great Britain is elected for a five-year term. However, at any time during those five years, the prime minister has the right to ask the monarch (the reigning king or queen) to dissolve the Parliament and call for a general election. A notice of only three weeks is all that is needed. So, if one party has been in control—the Conservatives, for example—for four years of a five-year term and they feel they are very popular at that point, they might call for a general election. Assuming they win, they would then have another five years to rule instead of the one remaining on the old term. Riding on the popularity of her stand on the Falklands, Margaret Thatcher took advantage of this right. She asked that Parliament be dissolved and a general election called in 1983. It was scheduled for June 9.

The Labour Party and Tony Blair were unhappy with the announcement. Thatcher's popularity seemed to guarantee a Conservative victory. In addition, the British public held the

The Way England Works

Once Blair decided to get involved in politics, it made sense for him to stand for Parliament, just as an American might run for the U.S. Congress. Aside from that similarity, the British government system operates quite differently than the system in the United States. The United Kingdom of Great Britain and Northern Ireland (UK), which includes England, Scotland, Wales, and Northern Ireland, is a constitutional monarchy. The monarch, currently Queen Elizabeth II, is the head of state but primarily carries out ceremonial duties. She is a symbol of national identity and unity. But over the years, as parliamentary democracy developed, the role and power of the monarch have greatly diminished.

The House of Commons has the real power in the modern UK. It is this body to which Blair was elected on his first step toward becoming prime minister. Commons has 659 members chosen by direct ballot. It alone has the power to impose taxes and to allocate money to government departments. Members are elected for five-year terms. Unlike in the United States, where the president is elected separately from the Congress, the head of the largest party in the House of Commons is generally designated the prime minister.

Labour Party responsible for a series of crippling union strikes (the party is deeply affiliated with the unions) that had badly affected the country in the late 1970s. Labour was sure to suffer in the voting booths.

Blair himself had even more troubles. Although the party leaders in Beaconsfield wanted him to stand again, some of his fellow party members advised him against it, pointing out that a Labour candidate simply did not have a chance in that Conservative stronghold. So, Blair had to look for a Labour seat elsewhere. Fortunately, after a series of political shake-ups and maneuverings, a Labour seat opened up in Sedgefield. The problem now was figuring out how Blair could become the candidate. He knew no one in Sedgefield.

To overcome this obstacle, Blair looked at the heart of the problem and devised the quickest and simplest way to solve it, an ability that marked his rise to power. Blair got a list of all affected districts and villages in the voting district of Sedgefield and found out that a village called Trimdon had not yet nominated a candidate. He called the village secretary, met with him and some of the other village Labour leaders, and was eventually nominated. This would not be the only time that Blair talked himself into getting what he wanted.

In all, there were seven nominations from various districts and villages for the Sedgefield seat. After five rounds of voting, Blair finally came out on top. He was now the Labour candidate from Sedgefield and eventually was elected to Parliament in the general election, with a majority of 8,281 votes from Sedgefield voters. At thirty years old, he became the youngest Labour member in Parliament.

Learning the Ropes

The year 1984 began Blair's upward political climb. It started on a happy personal note. The Blairs' first child, Euan John, was born on January 19, and the family moved into a large home, called Myrobella, in the center of the Sedgefield district. Cherie continued her active participation in Labour Party activities.

On the political side, Tony Blair was now in Parliament as a member of the Labour Party, but it was a party in crisis that desperately needed a boost in popularity. It also needed a new leader to help bring in new members. That leader was Neil Kinnock, elected as head of the Labour Party in October 1983, a job he would keep until 1992. Blair developed a close relationship with Kinnock over the years, which certainly helped his rapid rise through the party ranks. However, Blair did not succeed merely because of party affiliations. As quoted in *Current Leaders of Nations,* many observers gave most of the credit to Blair's "intelligence, energy, charm, and discipline."[14]

In late 1984, Kinnock promoted Blair to spokesperson for the opposition on treasury and economic affairs, a post he held until 1987. For the next several years, Blair made himself better known to his own party, to the Conservatives, and to the media. He was always unfailingly polite and agreeable, but people were most impressed by his keen understanding of complex issues. Blair was developing the character and personality that, years later, would cause a reporter for the *New Statesman* to say of him: "Nothing known about him gives us any good reason to doubt that he is what he seems to be. . . . His hair, his clothes, his

Neil Kinnock, head of the Labour Party, promoted Blair twice during his career.

friends and his opinions, his life as a proficient but not brilliant lawyer—what you see is what you get."[15]

In addition to his rise within the party ranks, Blair received both wanted and unwanted media attention during this period. In May 1985, he appeared on national television during an airing of the BBC's *Question Time,* a news program that highlights various members of Parliament or other political leaders. This kind of exposure was not often available to a young politician, and Blair was fortunate to get it. The press was also there to report the birth of the Blairs' second son, Nicholas Anthony.

In 1987, Kinnock gave Blair a new job as opposition spokesperson on trade and industry. He was also made deputy to Bryan Gould, who was the opposition trade and industry secretary. As Gould's deputy, Blair investigated the causes of the stock market crash in October 1987. In addition, he was responsible for consumer affairs and he oversaw many of the administrative duties of the city of London.

The year 1987 was also another election year. Although Blair won his seat in Sedgefield by a bigger majority than before, the election overall turned out to be another disaster for Labour. The Conservatives retained a large majority and Labour was still unpopular. The lost election forced Labour to consider reviewing its positions on such matters as defense and trade unions. Also, Labour was beginning to see how presentations on television and in front of the press could make it more popular. The Labour Party had to make its message seen and heard.

The Shadow Government

Within the party, Blair was also working hard to make himself seen and heard among its leaders. Overall, he had the support of those who counted. He continued to write newspaper articles on various issues and observations, keeping his name in front of his colleagues' noses. When he was not at work, Blair had a new interest at home. The Blairs' third child, and first daughter, Kathryn Hazel, was born on March 2, 1988.

In that year, Blair finally became part of the shadow cabinet as energy secretary. In Great Britain, the party that is not in

In 1988, Blair's daughter Kathryn (center) was born.

power—in other words, the one that does not hold the prime minister's post or the majority in Parliament—is known as the shadow government. The shadow government elects government officials (such as prime minister, energy secretary, and so forth) within the party as though it were in power. This way, the party out of power, also known as the opposition, is prepared for an actual takeover of government in the next election and ready to lead immediately.

As the shadow energy secretary, a position he held for one year, Blair developed an interest in conservation. He had seen in the elections that the British public was becoming increasingly concerned with conservation matters. Of particular concern were issues of air quality and the phenomenon of global warming. Although the environment never played an important role in later campaigns for Blair, his fight against the government's plan to privatize nuclear plants in 1989 led to another promotion.

The Unions

Blair was named shadow employment secretary in 1989, putting him in charge of a crucial matter for Labour: unemployment and the trade union law. Unemployment was rising in Britain, and much of the public blamed the trade unions because they had initiated crippling strikes over the past few years. Labour was viewed as the party of the unions, so the British people felt that the unions controlled the Labour Party.

As the new shadow employment secretary, Blair first tackled the problem of unemployment and the unions in a television program. He spoke in favor of a document called the Social Charter, which stated that employers and workers had the option of joining a professional organization or union. However, Labour had always advocated that workers be required to join a union, because nonunion workers could agree to work for lower salaries. That would threaten the salaries and jobs of working union members as well as jeopardize the union itself.

When asked if his statement meant a change in policy, Blair stumbled around without an answer. But once offscreen, he moved quickly. He called on each of the trade union leaders and told them, in effect, that a change that had been a long time com-

The Labour Party

The Labour Party, which Tony Blair joined in 1980, is one of the two major political parties in Great Britain. It grew out of a merger between the Trades Union Congress and the Independent Labour Party in 1900 and was named the Labour Representation Committee. The present name was adopted in 1906. With its strong links to the trade unions, the Labour Party grew rapidly. By 1918, Labour was the second largest party in the House of Commons, and when World War I ended, it became the official opposition party. Ramsey MacDonald was Labour's first prime minister, elected in 1924, but his government lasted only one year.

Britain's Labour Party is known for liberal, or left-wing, policies such as worldwide nuclear disarmament, union power, heavy taxation, and nationalization of key industries. Campaigning on a program of reconstruction and extended public welfare services after World War II, the party took over the government in 1945 and stayed in power for six years. It regained the majority in 1964 and then alternated with the Conservatives through the rest of the century. Since the 1980s, Labour has been moving more toward the political center on its fundamental issues and appealing more to the majority of voters.

ing needed to be made. He said that the practice of the closed shop, which required workers to be union members to get certain jobs, had to be eliminated. Belonging to a union could bring higher wages and certain other benefits such as faster promotion, but it was undemocratic, Blair said, that a worker be required to join a union if he or she did not wish to do so. In a firm but polite manner, he told the unions to do what was right and overdue.

It worked. The trade unions came around, all but one—the powerful NGA (National Graphical Association) print union. More than the other unions, the NGA wanted to keep the closed shop because it depended on it more heavily. However, the NGA eventually conceded, and the closed-shop policy was abandoned. Workers now had the right to choose whether or not to join a union. Labour was making a statement, a change, and Tony Blair was an important part of that.

The Election of 1992

Blair's stand concerning the trade unions had earned him respect, not only from the public but from his colleagues in the

House of Commons, the popularly elected body of the British Parliament. By 1992, Blair had become one of the most important figures in the shadow government. And as he became more comfortable with the television media, he learned to present himself as prepared, enthusiastic, and confident. He was poised for another step up in his rise to Labour Party leadership.

But for the moment, the upcoming general election was a more pressing problem. Once again, Blair campaigned for re-election to his parliamentary seat. Although he kept his seat in Sedgefield by a majority of 14,859 votes, Labour lost the majority in Parliament once again—the fourth defeat in a row. With the retirement of Margaret Thatcher, Conservative John Major became prime minister of Great Britain.

After the defeat, on April 10, 1992, Kinnock resigned from his position as leader of the Labour Party. He was succeeded by

Former President Bill Clinton (left) shakes hands with former British prime minister John Major (right). Major succeeded Margaret Thatcher as prime minister of Great Britain.

his deputy, and second in line, John Smith. Blair was urged by the party to run for the all-important position of Smith's deputy, a prestigious post. If Labour could win the next election, Smith would be prime minister and his deputy would be next in line. But Blair declined. It was rumored at the time that Blair did not want to fight his longtime colleague Gordon Brown for the post. Whether that was true or not, the position went to Margaret Beckett.

As leader, Smith gave Blair the position he wanted—shadow home secretary. The home secretary in the British government is the link between the monarch and the citizens of England and Wales and is in charge of internal affairs—security, crime, prisons, and illegal immigration.

Shadow Home Secretary

Blair's two years as shadow home secretary probably had the greatest impact on his political career, pushing him to the head of his party and eventually his country. Blair began his term as shadow home secretary by speaking about some of the British people's most pressing concerns, using each opportunity to criticize the Conservatives. For instance, concerning the rising crime rates in Great Britain, he accused the Conservatives of giving up on the problem. He said in a radio interview on January 10, 1993, "I think it's important that we are tough on crime and tough on the causes of crime too."[16] He went on to say that, although no one wanted to see an increase in the prison population, jailing more people might be necessary to combat the crime problem. Being tough on crime and its causes would be a recurring theme with Blair over the next two years.

For the most part, Blair was a liberal shadow home secretary, speaking out for civil rights and racial equality and against the death penalty. But Blair also edged closer to what many considered Conservative views. His "no tolerance on crime" stance strayed a bit from Labour policy.

Christian Socialism

As Blair spoke more and more to the British people, his politics became mixed with morality. He claimed that society had a moral obligation to give people a better life. In turn, the people had a responsibility to give back to the community by obeying its laws. Since these mutual responsibilities began with responsibility in the family, Blair believed that families must also be strengthened. Blair would continue this message into his post as prime minister. It was a good message because people listened and believed him. And it was good politics. It gave Blair reason and justification for his political actions. He said that, in order to fix what is wrong in the world, it is necessary to make judgments on what is good and bad. Blair called this belief "Christian socialism." Journalists began to call Blair a social moralist for the country.

The Reformer

Besides reforming the nation, Blair wanted to reform his own party by steering it toward Christian socialism. First, he began to concentrate on an issue called "one member, one vote," which meant that each member of the Labour Party should have a vote in the election of party leaders. Labour had always elected its leaders only from its MPs, or members of Parliament. The more liberal Labour members, including Blair, had been arguing for this change since 1982. It had been defeated then, but Blair was now determined to try again. However, before he had a chance, Labour had to deal with a more urgent matter.

On May 12, 1994, while on a campaign trip in Aberdeen, Blair got a shocking phone call: John Smith had had a fatal heart attack. The Labour Party was suddenly without a leader. Tony Blair decided to go after the party leadership. However, to do so, he would have to compete with his colleague Gordon Brown, who also wanted the position.

The British media favored Blair by a large margin, mainly citing his forceful stand on issues and his vote-getting personality. Many Labour members decided that it was more important to win the next general election, which they thought they could do with Blair, than to fight him on issues with which they disagreed. Blair won the position of party leader with a total of 57 percent of voting Labour party members. On July 21, 1994, Tony Blair became the youngest leader ever of Great Britain's Labour Party.

The unexpected death of Labour Party leader, John Smith, provided Blair an opportunity to stand for office.

After the election, Blair made an impassioned speech about his political ideals: "I meant what I said about wanting to win power, not to enjoy it, but to change the country, to change its place in the world, to make it a country people are proud of again, to make this country of ours a country where everyone gets the chance to succeed and get on." [17]

Tony Blair's rise to party leadership in just fourteen years was remarkable, but it was only half the dream. Though Blair was the head of a major party, the Labour Party was not in power. The prime minister of Great Britain was a Conservative, and the majority of voting members in the government were Conservative, not Labour. Blair was the head of only a shadow government. But he had come this far, and his mind was already fashioning the steps that would take Labour—and Tony Blair— to the top of Britain's political heap.

Chapter 3

The Race to the Top

From the moment he became head of the Labour Party in 1994, Tony Blair began work on a plan that would take him to the top political post of his country. He gave his party a new image and cast himself as the man who would modernize the British government. In the election of 1997, the people of Great Britain had a choice between Conservatives and Labour, a choice between John Major, the incumbent prime minister (the person already in office), or Tony Blair, the newcomer. For Blair to be the winner, Labour needed to win the election, meaning it had to gain a majority of seats in the House of Commons. Only with a Labour majority in Commons could Blair become prime minister. It was a huge challenge.

Although the press genuinely seemed to like Blair, many also believed he was nothing more than a charismatic politician who could talk his way into anything. They were aware of his quick rise through the party ranks and were not sure he had earned his position. Many members of the press, and some in his own party, doubted that Blair could pull it off. However, not only would Blair lead his party to victory in 1997, but it would be a landslide that would leave the Conservative Party stunned. For Blair and his shadow cabinet, it was a political work of art.

Blending the Old and New

Soon after being elected the opposition party leader, Blair showed his respect for centuries-old tradition by visiting the queen. He received a call from Buckingham Palace and was invited to a ceremony to be sworn in by the queen as a privy councillor. This is one of the highest honors Great Britain gives

Upon being elected head of the Labour Party, Blair proposed to modernize the British government. Here he stands with young Labour supporters.

to a politician. Centuries ago, the privy council was an active body composed of the monarch's personal advisers. Today, the privy council is a formality only, but it is an honor to be admitted to this inner circle.

Everyone attending the privy council ceremony must stand for its entire duration. Some say that the purpose is to make the ceremony as uncomfortable as possible. Others contend that it is to move matters along quickly so that the queen is not overly detained. After Elizabeth II bestows the honor on the new shadow prime minister, everyone attending walks out of the room backwards. If they cannot quite manage that, they execute a kind of sideways, crablike shuffle. The purpose of this strange behavior is to prevent turning one's back on the monarch even for a second, which, according to tradition, is very disrespectful. Blair got through the ceremony as though he had done it many times before.

Clause IV

With the privy council ceremony over, the new Labour leader faced a big challenge: getting the party back in power after eigh-

Queen Elizabeth II

Her official name is Elizabeth II, by the grace of God, of the United Kingdom of Great Britain and Northern Ireland and of her other realms and territories Queen, Head of the Commonwealth, Defender of the Faith. Tony Blair was not yet born when Elizabeth Alexandra Mary became queen of England on February 6, 1952. Elizabeth never expected to become queen because her father never expected to become king. She was the elder child of Albert, the duke of York, and Lady Elizabeth Bowes-Lyon, the "Queen Mum," who died on March 30, 2002. Albert, being a younger son, had little thought of becoming king, since that is the role for the oldest son in a family. But in 1936, his oldest brother, Edward VIII, suddenly gave up his throne for the divorced woman he loved and later married. This made Elizabeth's father the new monarch, who took the name of George VI. It also changed her future. She married Prince Philip of Greece and Denmark in 1947. They had four children: Charles in 1948, Anne in 1950, Andrew in 1960, and Edward in 1964. When her father died in 1952, Elizabeth took the throne.

Queen Elizabeth II waves from her carriage.

teen years of Conservative dominance. Labour had to concentrate on winning the most votes in the House of Commons. And winning a Labour victory in the next general election would mean the prime minister's post for Blair.

Blair's plan for victory called for a new party image. He wanted Labour to be seen by the voters as a new party, a modern party. The first step in changing the image was to give Labour a new name. Now it was to be called New Labour, and as stated in *Why Labour Won the General Election of 1997,* making New Labour "a new party was the core, the absolute heart, of Labour's strategy." [18]

One of the first steps in the makeover was to ditch the old Clause IV of the party's constitution. Clause IV had for centuries tagged Labour as the party that advocated common ownership, an economic system in which the government controls and distributes economic resources. This system is opposed to capitalism, such as that practiced in the United States, in which most of the means of production are privately owned. Common ownership of goods and production, however, had no place in Blair's view of modern government. According to public opinion polls, it was not favored by the British people either. There had been some attempts in the past eighteen years to get rid of or modify Clause IV, but to no avail. Now, Blair decided to tackle the issue. If the British people were to be convinced that New Labour was indeed a new party, then changing Clause IV was vital.

It was early in Blair's leadership of the party to take such a risky position. Most of the Labour officials did not want the clause changed because they felt it was symbolic of the party's history and roots. And many members were reluctant to take on the task of reworking or rewriting it. But Blair was persistent. At the Scottish Labour Party conference in March 1995 in Inverness, he spoke passionately to his audience about the need for change in the modern world. At the national executive meeting a few days later, he presented a new Clause IV, the outline of which he had scribbled on a flight from Glasgow to London. The new clause was not entirely different; it merely diluted the words of the old clause, removing a direct reference to common ownership.

Meet the Conservatives

The formal name of the Conservative Party in Great Britain is the National Union of Conservative and Unionist Associations. Its members are also known as Tories. They evolved from the old Tory Party of 1832. Sir Robert Peel was the first Conservative prime minister in 1834.

The Tories, or Conservatives, are mainly comprised of middle-class voters. Only about 20 percent of the working class belongs to the party, although the Tories have often been supported by workers in general elections. The Conservative members of Parliament tend to be lawyers, landowners, company heads, and publishers. Known as a right-of-center political party, the Conservatives dominated British politics for much of the twentieth century. They stress law and order, the importance of land ownership, an orderly system of taxation, and social reform.

The party eventually approved the new clause. The old traditions of the philosophy of common ownership were changed, and the new Clause IV now represented a new party. It indicated that Labour was taking its place in the modern world behind a modern leader.

Building the New Image

Blair now led a party with a new name and a new clause, but there was far more to be done. New strategies needed to be put in place to establish an effective campaign that would bring the new image to the public eye. Labour decided on several approaches.

First, Labour planned to step into what had become the Conservative Party's territory. In its campaigns, Labour would sell itself as the party of family, business, and responsibility. This tied in with Blair's philosophy of Christian socialism. Second, the party would pride itself on being trustworthy on all issues. To Blair, that meant thinking through an issue, making a decision, and then standing firm behind that choice. Third, when the Labour Party disagreed with the Conservatives, Labour would stay on the attack—through speeches in Commons or reports in the press—until the issue was resolved. Finally, Labour would stop discussing taxes as a primary issue. Labour leaders were convinced that one of the main reasons they had lost the last election was because of their position on taxes.

Everyone knew, or thought they knew, that if Labour took power, taxes would be increased—at least for the rich. Labour leaders had indicated as much over the past several years as a way to right many of the internal problems of the country. The Conservatives certainly assumed that Labour would raise taxes. They had launched a poster campaign that said "You can't trust Labour," referring to the tax issue. The Conservative campaign was effective, and the general public again started to grumble about the possibility of a tax hike. However, Blair quickly offset the Conservatives with a statement on the subject. He initiated a poster campaign of his own that showed Blair, his signature, and a pledge card that stated, "No rises in income tax rates." The message was that, under no circumstances, would the Labour Party raise income taxes if it gained control of Parliament.

Blair's Personality and Image

When Blair began to build a new image for the Labour Party, he knew that he, as the party leader, would be an important part of that image. Voters might very well decide issues on how he campaigned, how he presented himself, and how much they believed in what he said. Thus, Blair's own personality would be a strong factor in victory.

Blair is known for his winning personality, charm, and easy smile. He appears neither complacent nor arrogant in his speeches. Whether on television or meeting face to face with the public, he rarely uses the type of language that politicians typically employ to impress an audience. During interviews, he usually sounds like any Englishman one might encounter on the street.

Those who know Tony Blair well say he is open to new ideas and suggestions, which is an asset for a politician. He also has a tough inner strength and great self-confidence. That self-confidence helps him to act decisively once he has set his mind on a goal. He will let nothing—and sometimes no one—stand in his way if he is doing what he is convinced is right.

Some of Blair's perspective on personal image was influenced by Bill Clinton, the forty-second president of the United States, who is also an effective and charismatic speaker. After

Clinton entered the White House, Blair made several trips to
the United States and the two men became good friends.

Learning New Methods

During his search for a new party image, Blair was especially interested in studying the methods that Clinton's campaign leaders had used in 1992 to defeat the incumbent Republican
president, George Bush. Blair had members of Labour set up
contacts with the Clinton administration to foster a working ex-
change of ideas. Blair had a lot to learn from Clinton, who had
also been a modernizer for his party. Clinton had led the Demo-
cratic Party toward social change and sold that message to the
people. Blair learned that the Democrats did not win the election by appealing to their traditional interest groups, but by
making a broad appeal to all groups. So, Blair believed, Labour
could not win just by appealing to its traditional interest groups,
such as the disabled or unemployed. The message had to be
broader and all-inclusive; Labour had to campaign on middle
ground. Blair now had his campaign message. He would speak
out as the leader of a party that had transformed itself into a

*Blair with President Clinton (second from right), Hillary Clinton
(far left) and Cherie Blair in front of London's Tower Bridge.*

modern organization capable of satisfying the needs of a modern country.

Using the Media

The campaign began on March 17, 1997, when Prime Minister John Major formally asked Queen Elizabeth II to dissolve Parliament and order a general election, set for May 1. Although Blair sensed that the country's mood was shifting toward Labour, he anticipated a tough and close campaign. But no matter what the polls showed, he was not going to stop working until victory had been declared. In several elections over the past decades, Labour had been accused of not campaigning hard enough because the polls indicated that it was the party in favor at the time. Blair was determined not to let overconfidence ruin another chance for a Labour victory.

After the Easter break, the business of campaigning really got started. Three buses with Blair campaign slogans set out across Britain, and Blair showed up at various locations to deliver speeches to the crowds. The election was also fought in large measure, as most modern elections are, in the television studios.

Borrowing from Bill Clinton's successful campaigns, Alastair Campbell and Peter Mandelson, two of Blair's close advisers and media specialists, set up a giant media room. Television, radio, and press outlets were monitored twenty-four hours a day, staffed by a team of 150 people. The team expanded as the election date approached. If someone campaigning for Labour was criticized for a particular statement, the media room knew about it right away and could quickly repair the damage. If something was said by a Conservative that needed an instant rebuttal, the media room found the facts for the next speech.

Well before the actual campaigning, the Labour Party tried to turn every small happening into a bigger event worth noting in the press. If a Conservative member of Parliament gave a speech on a plan to improve the transportation system, three Labour leaders would give three speeches on how the Conservatives had ruined the system in the first place. Whatever cast the Conservatives in a bad light was considered fair game. As the weeks went on, Conservative prime minister John Major became increasingly

Conservative John Major

John Major has been a leading figure in Great Britain's Conservative Party since 1979. The son of a circus performer, he left school at age sixteen to help support his family. After working as an accountant for some years, he tried twice—unsuccessfully—to stand for a seat in Parliament in 1974. But with the Conservative landslide victory in 1979, Major gained a seat in the House of Commons and climbed rapidly in his party's ranks, much as Blair did in the Labour Party. And like Blair, Major was helped by the personal backing of his party's leader, in this case Prime Minister Margaret Thatcher. Under her government, Major was named junior minister in 1986, chief secretary to the treasury in 1987, foreign secretary in 1989, and a few months later chancellor of the exchequer, in charge of the country's finances.

When Thatcher unexpectedly resigned in November 1990, Major won a three-way contest for the prime minister and became head of the British government on November 28, 1990. A downturn in the economy and rise in the crime rate helped to bring about the public disillusionment with his Conservative policies. Major lost the role of prime minister to Blair in 1997 but remains the head of his party.

annoyed at Labour's success in taking press attention away from any accomplishments by the government in power.

Major was not the only one who was annoyed. The Conservative members of Parliament were also irritated at the smoothness of the Labour media blitz. It seemed as though if Labour repeated something enough times, it got printed and was soon accepted as fact. As Blair said, "In politics, you have to restate a message a thousand times before even a small fraction of people hear it." [19] One of the things that Labour kept repeating was what the polls were already showing: Labour was in the lead.

The Conservatives did not help their cause much by fighting among themselves. They worried about their hands-off policy toward Europe. The Conservative Party had maintained a cautious stance regarding becoming allied in a closer union with other European countries. Now, when it seemed as though the British people were more willing to consider a closer relationship, some Conservatives questioned their own party's position. And Conservatives disagreed with each other over what to do about their declining popularity. This infighting only served the Labour conviction—which Labour broadcast as loudly and as often as it could—that the British public would be foolish to trust a fifth term in power to such a disorganized group. "It is time for a change," said every Labour poster. "Enough is enough," shouted every Labour speaker. This effective use of the media is a main reason for Labour's success in the 1997 campaign.

Blair's Growing Confidence

Also growing during the election campaign was Tony Blair's confidence level. Earlier in the year, on April 7, he had made a television appearance on a program called *Panorama,* during which he answered questions. He appeared quite nervous and was slow in responding with decisive answers. But by April 24,

Nervous about speaking publicly, Blair practiced and became more confident. Here he speaks during a rally in London.

on another news program called *Question Time,* he was self-assured and almost aggressive with his responses. His confidence was evident when he stated, "There is a word in the English language and it's called no, and if people make demands upon me that I think are wrong then they'll be refused."[20]

The Candidates

Confidence is one of many traits that voters look for in a candidate in any election. In the 1997 election campaign, which to some extent boiled down to the characters of the men who might be prime minister, the press had much to say for the voters to judge. And most of what the newspapers printed was about Blair.

Of the nine major newspapers in Great Britain, six of them backed the Labour Party and three were pro-Conservative. Even though Blair had no experience with a government in power, the pro-Labour papers delighted in discussing his leadership or anything at all that would keep his name in the press, even if they criticized him. This served to present Blair as a very human

John Major waves to a crowd. Major stood against Tony Blair in the 1997 election for prime minister.

figure in the eyes of the public. Though referring to Major as a decent man, both the Labour and Conservative press cast doubts on his leadership abilities. In fact, Major was described by one newspaper as "a decent man who does his best" but "so weak he could not run a bath."[21] In contrast, even the Conservative press had some praise for Blair. Papers such as the *Daily Telegraph* and *Daily Mail* applauded his passion for what he believes in and his determination. However, they also said he was "untrustworthy, unprincipled, and evasive."[22]

In general, though, Blair became the darling of the press. The *Sun* editorials were especially laudatory, calling him "a man with vision and courage—with the makings of a great Prime Minister."[23] He was hailed as being a dynamic leader and the best man for the post. The headline in the *Sun* on the day after the election date was announced, March 18, 1997, read: "The *Sun* Backs Blair. Give change a chance."[24] The *Sun* was backing not the change in Labour but Tony Blair's bringing about the capability of change that was promised. The pro-Labour press believed that changes were needed in the country and that Tony Blair was a tough, determined reformer.

Eager-to-Please Blair

Blair helped his favorable press image during the six weeks of the 1997 campaign by being seen just about everywhere. He was a candidate who was eager to please. In fact, during this period, an American journalist interviewed Blair at his Myrobella home and after the meeting said, "I've interviewed some of the world's most extraordinary people in my professional life. . . . Never have I come across anybody quite . . . as eager to please as Tony Blair."[25] In addition to formal interviews, Blair made sure he was seen and read about elsewhere. He smiled from an article in a women's magazine with his beloved guitar in hand as he spoke of the Beatles and the rock 'n' roll generation. He was quoted in an article on museums in which he discussed his favorite artists. He also admitted that he played the lottery once in a while, using his children's birth dates for the numbers. Blair was very effective in portraying himself as being much like the average British citizen.

Sometimes, however, the press coverage on Blair was negative, such as when rumors circulated that Blair was wearing a small earpiece so he could be prompted during interviews or speeches. This implied that he was not capable enough or well versed enough to speak on his own. Even though no such earpiece ever turned up, the rumors bothered Blair so much that sometimes he even stopped using a teleprompter, a rolling screen that speakers commonly read from when delivering long speeches. When Blair was really at his best, he simply shed his jacket, rolled up his sleeves, threw his prepared speech aside, and spoke to the people. Those performances—perhaps a little like his old drama days at Fettes—received the best reviews.

The British people also liked seeing Blair with his wife, Cherie, and the children during the campaign. The Blair family was often in the media during those weeks. In fact, no other politician in British memory had so used his or her family in that way. Blair was seen on one TV broadcast helping his children with their homework. If the children were not alongside him, he referred to them frequently in his speeches. He referred to himself often and earnestly as a family man, which he still does. He once told an interviewer that children "drive you mad but keep you sane" and that "I think I function better as a politician because I lead such a normal life."[26] There was some mild criticism about Blair exposing his family too much while campaigning, and Blair himself expressed worry about any possible harm to the children. However, he also said that Cherie had told him she wanted the family to be a part of the election process.

Election Day—May 1, 1997

Finally, after all the campaigning was over, the only thing Blair could do was wait for the results. When the final tally was in, Labour had won the election with 419 seats, a majority of 179. This gave Labour a greater majority than any party had had since 1935. The Conservatives took only 165 seats, their lowest share since 1832. The Liberal Democrats got 46 seats. It was a landslide for Labour and a sad day for the Conservatives. John Major called Blair at the Constituency Labour Club in Trimdon to say he was conceding the election.

Blair waves to supporters during a victory rally at the Royal Festival Hall in London.

At about 5:00 A.M. on the morning of May 2, Blair, his wife, and his closest advisers arrived at the Royal Festival Hall in London. Accepting victory, Blair made a short speech, saying, "We have been elected as New Labour and we will govern as New Labour."[27]

A few days short of his forty-fourth birthday, Anthony Charles Lynton Blair became Great Britain's youngest prime minister since Lord Liverpool in 1812. But even in that glorious moment of victory, Blair knew a challenge lay ahead: He had promised a New Labour Party, and the British public would expect him to deliver.

Chapter 4

Blair's Personal Life

Publicly, Prime Minister Tony Blair is charming and outgoing. But he is also a private man who prefers to keep his family, his religion, and his personal feelings in the background as much as possible. As the leader of a major world power who wants to take his country in new directions, privacy is not always feasible. Blair relies on his spiritual values and his sense of honesty to see him through both the political and private sides of his life.

Blair and his family acknowledge a crowd. For the most part, Blair prefers to keep his private life separate from his public life.

A Family Man

Any politician faces certain challenges in trying to maintain a balance between political and private life. Blair realized this as a boy, for his father's political ambitions kept him away from home much of the time. That is probably part of the reason, as the British press has commented, that Blair spends more personal time with his family than any prime minister before him. He is an active father. Although he is very busy, he has been known to take time out to make his children's breakfast or walk them to school.

Blair often praises the value of family life in his public life as well. "It is within the family that we learn that there is such a thing as society," he said in a speech in Cape Town, South Africa, in 1996, "and it is upon the values of the extended family that the decent society will be built."[28] Blair believes that the family must be the foundation for a modern Britain.

The Prime Minister's Wife

Even a close family such as the prime minister's has at times drawn criticism from the British people and press. The criticism mostly centered on Cherie Blair. As soon as Tony Blair decided to stand for the 1997 election, questions began about whether Cherie would or should be a full-time prime minister's wife or a full-time lawyer. In fact, she remains one of London's most respected lawyers. She was awarded the title of queen's counsel at the age of forty, which is very young for such an honor. Members of the Queen's Counsel are appointed by the Lord Chancellor, the head of Britain's court system, and rank higher than regular members of the bar. Because queen's counsellors wear silk court gowns rather than cloth ones, when they are appointed, they are said to be "taking silk." In 1996, Cherie Blair was also named Britain's Legal Personality of the Year by the *Lawyer* magazine, the first time the title was given to a woman. Cherie has made it very clear how she feels about her work. During the elections, she was asked by a reporter if she planned to give up her job if Blair became prime minister. Cherie replied, "And can you tell me one good reason why I should?"[29]

Shortly after the Blairs moved to the prime minister's residence, Cherie was back at work at her labor and administrative law practice. She is also a part-time junior judge. Many prime ministers in Britain have had very powerful and influential wives, but Cherie Blair is the first "first lady" in the nation's history to maintain a serious career.

Although Blair's wife has always backed him completely in politics, she is not entirely comfortable with the media scrutiny that goes along with being a member of the prime minister's family. Cherie once said to a reporter, "I'm not a clotheshorse or a frilly person. I live in the real world most of the time."[30] But Cherie Blair's "real world" has changed since her husband became prime minister. When the press found out that she was visiting a gym three times a week supposedly to improve her appearance, the *Daily Telegraph* said, "One need only imagine

Cherie Blair wears a traditional barrister's wig when she practices law.

Cherie Blair in the Spotlight

Cherie Blair is a top-rated lawyer who has always wholeheartedly backed her husband's campaigns, but she does not welcome the spotlight. Whereas Tony Blair is naturally easygoing and glib when necessary, Cherie is often impatient with what she considers irrelevant questions. For the most part, however, she has stood up well to them. She is frequently asked if she makes more money than her husband. Her answer is a direct "yes." In fact, Cherie was the family breadwinner for many years while Blair was a fledgling in politics. Cherie Blair is also an expert at juggling her time. Soon after the family had moved into the prime minister's home on Downing Street, she was already back at work in her law offices, where she usually works five days a week.

Generally straightforward and direct when dealing with the public and the press, Cherie on occasion has given some insight into domestic situations in the Blair household. For example, she acknowledges that the prime minister is often helpful around the house and even occasionally cooks. However, she says that he has no working knowledge of a washing machine.

Mary Wilson [wife of former Labour prime minister Harold Wilson] submitting to the demands of a fitness trainer to grasp how much the demands of a Labour leader's wife have changed over a single generation."[31]

Cherie Blair has many of the same qualities attributed to her husband. She is forceful and determined, intelligent, and well spoken. Her politics are similar to Blair's, and if anything, she is said to be more liberal. Perhaps because she so dislikes being in the public eye, in the early years she tended to be somewhat severe in appearance and manner. But, as she has grown more comfortable with the constant scrutiny, Historian David Starkey says of her, she seems to have softened. "She's a barrister, she's a lawyer, she's a very good actress."[32] Said her law partner Michael Beloff, "She looks fragile, but she's got a character of steel."[33]

Life on Downing Street

Cherie Blair has become used to change since she married Tony Blair. One of the biggest changes occurred shortly after the 1997 election when the family moved into the prime minister's official

London home at number 10 Downing Street. Actually, the Blairs
live in the larger flat, or apartment, on the second floor of numbers 10 and 11 Downing Street, just as the U.S. president lives
on the second floor of the White House and his office is on the
ground floor. Number 10 alone is not big enough for the children. The two houses that make up numbers 10 and 11 were
joined in 1732 when the property became the official government residence. Before the Blairs' move, a reporter for the *New
Statesman* wondered "whether [Prime Minister Margaret] Thatcher's 'flat above the shop' will suitably accommodate a working couple, three children and an electric guitar."[34] Even with
more room, it takes time to adjust to life at Downing Street because it is always very busy and very professional. But the Blairs
decided to live at the official residence (rather than their London house in Richmond Crescent) so that, while working, Blair
would be able to have more private time with his family.

The Blairs' private life began to be made public when they
moved into the Downing Street house. Reporters and photogra-

*Two men guard the entrance to 10 Downing Street, the prime minister's
office and living quarters.*

Britain's White House

The prime minister of Great Britain lives at number 10 Downing Street in London, England, just as the president of the United States lives in the White House at 1600 Pennsylvania Avenue in Washington, D.C. Both of them live above their offices. Downing Street did not become the official prime minister's residence until 1902. Before that, some prime ministers chose to live there and some did not.

There have been many changes to the prime minister's residence through the years to accommodate personal tastes and changing living styles. Electricity was installed in 1894, and telephones soon after. In the early 1990s, computer cabling arrived at number 10.

The official residence is close to the site of what was once the palace of Whitehall, which was the official residence of the reigning monarch until it was destroyed by fire in 1698. All that remains is the Banqueting House, which is open to visitors.

phers documented their intimate possessions as they were transferred from one location to the other. Suits and dresses and children's clothes went out of their home on wire hangers and traveled to Downing Street in a few vans. The moving in and out went on for much of the day. A month later, the cameras also caught a Swedish-made bed being delivered to the prime minister's residence. Said the headline in the *Sun,* "Things can only get bedder."[35]

It was this media scrutiny that made the Blairs decide to sell the house in Richmond Crescent, although they kept Myrobella in the Sedgefield district. They had initially thought that they would keep a second London home as well, but they soon realized that all the security restrictions would encroach on their neighbors' sense of privacy. The sale of the house came just in time for Blair to be hit with his own party's stamp duty (property sales tax) on houses worth over 250,000 pounds, which was imposed in the first Labour budget.

The Blair Children

In addition to the normal curiosity about the new prime minister's wife and where they would live, there was also much interest in the couple's three children, ages thirteen, eleven, and nine

Tony and Cherie Blair try their best to keep their children out of the spotlight. Here, Blair is seen holding his fourth child Leo George Blair.

in 1997. Blair was the first prime minister in the twentieth century to have elementary-age schoolchildren. Before the move to Downing Street, with Cherie working full-time, the Blair children had been cared for by a nanny. Blair's brother and sister and Cherie's sister, Lyndsey, who lived close by, were also often called in to help.

Both Blair and his wife understand that everything their children do will be under scrutiny while he is in office. For example, their eldest son, Euan, got a bit part in the opera *Turandot* by Puccini, performed at the Royal Opera House. A story the next day in the *Telegraph* questioned how the family felt having their son appearing in an opera with fascist overtones (the chorus of the opera seems to praise what became the dictatorship of Benito Mussolini in Italy).

However, for the most part, the Blairs have been successful in keeping their children out of the spotlight. But on May 20, 2000, they could not exclude the press from the birth of their fourth child, Leo George Blair. Leo's birth caused quite a stir; he was the first child born to a prime minister in office in 150 years.

On the Tuesday before Leo's birth, Cherie was still in her office busy challenging her husband's government on the subject of parental leave from work. She claimed that the thirteen weeks' leave given only to parents whose children were born after December 15, 1999, was unfair. She said it unlawfully excluded millions of parents from taking time off to be with their families. In answer to her challenge, the judge said they would rule on the issue the following week. Mrs. Blair, who expected to be in the hospital that week delivering her baby, responded, "I hope your lordships will excuse me if I am not available." [36] The prime minister had no comment on his wife's challenge.

However, after Leo's birth, Blair did get involved in a parental leave controversy of sorts. Because he often refers to himself as a modern family man, his wife suggested that he be the one to take the leave of absence from work to be with the infant during the first few weeks. The press discussed the idea for a few days, but ultimately Blair continued working. He did, however, take a two-week vacation/paternity leave after the birth and promised to ease up on his official workload for a while. He also speculated that he would be up late at night at home. Said the new father, "Cherie has many excellent qualities, but once she goes to sleep, it takes a minor nuclear explosion to wake her up." [37]

Children in the News

Even before Leo's birth, Blair began to change his policy about exposing his family to the media. He stopped talking about them so often in public. Although he had always been concerned about their security, he grew more so. He does allow them to be photographed at the start of family holidays. However, he now insists that the press adhere to the established Code of Conduct in Great Britain. The code states that children are not to be photographed or interviewed if the only reason for such is that they have famous parents. In other words, except for stated times, the child of a famous parent should be photographed only if what he or she does is considered newsworthy.

Such was the case, at least as far as the press saw it, in July 2000, when sixteen-year-old Euan Blair was arrested by police

for being intoxicated in London's Leicester Square. In addition
to being under eighteen, the legal drinking age in Great Britain,
Euan gave the police a false name and birth date and said he was
celebrating the end of exams. The boy was not charged but was
ordered to report to police at a later date for possible action. Only
a few days earlier, Euan's father had promised the British people
that he was going to toughen the existing laws against intoxica-
tion. The embarrassment for the prime minister was noted by
the press. Said a spokesperson for the family, "Euan is very sorry
for the inconvenience he caused to the police, the state he was
in, and for the false statement that he made. He is in no doubt of
the seriousness of it and the view that his parents take of it." [38]
The view that Euan's parents took of the incident was clear in
the distressed look on Blair's face the next time he appeared on
television. However, his very real parental reaction elicited a
sympathetic response from the British people. Blair seemed less
like a prime minister and more like one of them, an ordinary person grappling with a familiar domestic problem.

These qualities about Tony Blair help the British public re-
late to him as a person even if they do not always agree with his
policies. They like the fact that he enjoys his children and is as
comfortable discussing a needed diaper change for Leo as he is
discussing the methods by which his Labour government will
upgrade the British education system.

Religion

Another part of Tony Blair's life that is very important to him is
his religion. He feels that his faith is a private matter, but he is
not reluctant to talk about it. The role religion plays in his day-
to-day life is evident to the public.

Blair belongs to the Church of England, although he attends
Catholic services with his wife and children, who belong to the
Catholic Church. Blair feels that it is important for the family to
worship together, but sees no reason to give up the Church of
England and has no plans to convert to Catholicism.

According to records, Blair is the first prime minister since
William Ewart Gladstone, who was in office four times between
1868 and 1894, to make a habit of reading the Bible. Blair says

Muslims in Great Britain

Muslims in Great Britain, as elsewhere, follow strict principles based on religious values and the teachings of their holy book, the Koran. The Muslim religion is based on five principles of Islam: A statement of faith must be recited; five prayers are made at specific times each day, usually at the mosque, the Muslim place of worship; a portion of one's earnings must be donated to charity; during the season of Ramadan, the faithful must fast from sunset to sundown; and at some point in one's life, a pilgrimage should be made to the holy site of Mecca, located in western Saudi Arabia.

The approximately 1.5 million Muslims who live in Great Britain today often have difficulty following the dictates of their religion. For instance, according to the Islamic faith, girls are supposed to cover their heads with a scarf. Most schools in Britain do not allow that. Although there are many mosques, in Great Britain, the majority of Muslims cannot attend them regularly because of their jobs. Muslims also are typically divided by nationality, class, and religious traditions. Islamic organizations in Great Britain have had little success in unifying the various Muslim communities and enacting laws that would integrate the followers of Islam more effectively into British life.

of his faith, "Christianity is a very tough religion. It is judgemental. There is right and wrong. There is good and bad. We all know this, of course, but it has become fashionable to be uncomfortable about such language."[39] Blair is familiar with other religions, too. He has read the Koran, the Muslim holy book, at least three times and agrees with the Muslim concepts of love and fellowship.

He Is What He Is

Blair has been in the prime minister's office long enough for admirers and critics alike to have figured him out—or at least to think they have. An article in the *New Statesman* in October 2002 described Blair as a shock to modern politics—he simply is what he is. Says author Julian Glover, "[The old political joke says] 'These are my principles, and if you don't like them I have others.' . . . But if you don't like Tony Blair's principles, he doesn't have any others. Blair is what he is. It is little short of shocking."[40] At first glance, that seems true. Blair is from the prosperous middle class and he never denies it. He is a good—but not

Blair and his wife pray during a special service honoring September 11 victims.

outstanding—lawyer and never has claimed to be otherwise. He really believes he is a straightforward, honest guy.

His critics, however, say that that "straightforward, honest guy" is just a facade. They claim he is a determined, even ruthless politician who will do whatever it takes to get what he wants. He has been accused by his critics of not leading the government but dictating it. As quoted in the *New Statesman,* "Blair has projected himself as the true voice of the British people."[41]

The debate continues over the driven public politician and the private man behind the charming smile. In the meantime, the prime minister keeps on being both. He rarely responds to his critics and has often said that he will continue to act in a way he believes is best for his country, his family, and himself. However he acts, he knows that almost anything he does is open for comment. Like any politician or well-known figure, Tony Blair spends most of his life, at work or at home, in a very public world.

Chapter 5

A New Look for the New Century

Tony Blair, who was elected to a second term as prime minister in 2001, wants to lead a modernized Great Britain into the twenty-first century. There is no doubt that both he and the British government have a new look in the eyes of the world since he took office in 1997. But Blair has still not convinced the British people to join in a closer union with the rest of Europe, and he has not yet brought about promised reforms in education, transportation, and health care. His second term will prove his abilities as Great Britain's leader of the twenty-first century.

Blair and Cherie walk to Buckingham Palace after his reelection as prime minister in 2001.

Blair and the Monarchy

Tony Blair, a twenty-first-century leader, seems comfortable operating within the centuries-old, tradition-bound protocol of his country. He follows the traditions easily. With just a few hours' rest after his initial election, he went straight to Buckingham Palace, where, as quoted in *Tony Blair: Prime Minister,* he accepted "Her Majesty the Queen's kind offer to form a new administration of government in this country."[42] As an Englishman, Blair has no deep-rooted attachment to the monarchy, yet he has continued a close relationship with Elizabeth II. On the anniversary of the queen's fifty years on the throne in June 2002, he spoke in her honor at the Guild Hall, with Elizabeth attending.

Handling a Tragedy

Blair's actions following the tragic death of Princess Diana shortly after he became prime minister not only showed deep empathy for the monarchy but raised his personal esteem with the British people. Blair was never more charismatic or moving than during his television appearance just hours after Diana was killed in a car crash in Paris on August 31, 1997. The former wife of the queen's son and heir, Prince Charles, Diana had been a great favorite with the British people, who were deeply shaken by the news.

Blair got the news of Diana's death in the early morning hours at his Myrobella home. He was scheduled to attend church in Sedgefield that morning and he knew the television cameras would be there. But Blair had no black tie or cufflinks with him at Myrobella. He borrowed a black tie from one of his aides and phoned another for cufflinks. Thus suitably attired, a somber prime minister, just four months in office, appeared before the cameras to speak to a nation in shock.

"I feel like everyone else in this country today," he said. "I am utterly devastated. . . . People everywhere, not just here in Britain, kept faith with Princess Diana. They liked her, they loved her, they regarded her as one of the people. She was the people's princess and that is how she will stay, how she will remain in our hearts and our memories for ever."[43] The country seemed comforted by Blair's understanding, sympathetic words, and they helped to unite a saddened people.

The People's Princess

Diana Frances Spencer married Charles, Prince of Wales and heir to the British throne, on July 29, 1981, thus granting her the title of Princess of Wales. She grew up at Park House, a home her parents rented on the estate of Queen Elizabeth II, and her playmates were the queen's younger sons, Prince Andrew and Edward. She became Lady Diana Spencer when her father became an earl in 1975. After finishing school in Switzerland, Diana returned to England and became a kindergarten teacher. At that time, she renewed contacts with the royal family, which eventually led to her marriage to Charles. Diana and Charles had two sons, Prince William Arthur Philip Louis, second heir to the throne, in 1982 and Prince Henry Charles Albert David in 1984. The marriage, however, was troubled and ended in divorce in 1996.

Britain and the world were shocked when Diana was killed in a tragic car accident in Paris in the early morning hours of August 31, 1997. She and Dodi al-Fayed, the son of an Egyptian tycoon, left the Ritz Hotel at 12:15 A.M. in a black Mercedes driven by hotel chauffeur Henri Paul. Also with them was Diana's bodyguard, Trever Rees-Jones. As Paul was speeding through the Alma tunnel, the car was struck by another vehicle. Rees-Jones was the only survivor.

Diana, Princess of Wales.

In the coming weeks, the sadness over Diana's death and the subdued mood of the nation created a bond between the Labour Party and the monarchy. Blair's public relations people handled events for the royal family. (Many Britons believed that the queen and other members of the royal family had treated Diana harshly during her lifetime. It was said that the queen often disapproved of Diana's globe-trotting and blamed her for the divorce from Charles the year before her death.) Blair also presented himself as a kind of spokesman for the monarchy. He

Pallbearers carrying Princess Diana's casket in 1997. Blair read a passage from the Bible at her funeral.

was present when Diana's body was flown back from France, and he read a passage from the Bible at her funeral in Westminster Abbey. When Diana's family wanted a private funeral, Blair made sure that the government ensured their privacy. Some critics said his behavior was politically motivated, and indeed Blair did receive much public praise for his actions, but most believe he was genuinely saddened by the event.

Building a Government

Riding on a wave of popularity during those first months in office, Blair set about the business of forming a government. He was well aware that all of his cabinet ministers had served only in a shadow government. He was also aware that he was the first prime minister since 1924 to take office without holding any posts in an existing government.

Blair was a busy prime minister. No detail seemed too small for his attention. As a Parliament member, he had occasionally attended the customary "prime minister's questions," twice-weekly sessions of fifteen minutes each. During those sessions, the leader of the opposition party fired off whatever questions he or she chose, plus questions from other members of Parliament if there was time. The prime minister could ask only three questions of the opposition and had no idea what he or she would be asked. Blair remembered it as a harrowing experience, even when he was the one doing the questioning. So, when he became prime minister, he changed the format to one 30-minute question-and-answer period a week. It was still terrifying, but at least it was only once a week.

As part of his desire to bring Great Britain into a closer union with Europe, Blair also signed the European Social Chapter published by the European Commission. Great Britain is a member of the European Union (EU), formerly the Common Market. The EU is an organization of European countries joined for economic benefit. It has eased travel restrictions among the nations, made laws more compatible, and allowed for a quicker, less complicated flow of economic goods and services among

Britons Resist the Euro

The results of polls conducted in June and August 2002 show that as many as 75 percent of the British people do not want to adopt the euro, Europe's universal currency. The euro was launched in January 1999 as an electronic currency, and euro notes and coins came into circulation on January 1, 2002. The euro is now the currency of eleven of the fifteen members of the European Union; only Luxembourg, Greece, Sweden, and the United Kingdom do not use it. The new currency is intended to make financial dealings easier and more stabilized through Europe (and for the millions of visitors who flock to these countries each year).

Blair and his government favor British adoption of the euro. He feels that Britain will face economic problems if it does not join the system. Critics say that Britain does not need the euro as it is enjoying a period of economic stability. If the euro fails, so will the British economy. The British public's bias against the euro also seems based on an unwillingness to part with the pound, which has been the English currency standard for centuries. Economic experts expect that there will be a referendum in Great Britain put before the people on the issue of whether or not to accept the euro by the year 2004.

the member countries. However, Great Britain has not joined the European Monetary Union (EMU), which standardizes money throughout the EU. Members of the EMU have converted their currency to the euro as the common financial basis. This is a touchy point with the English public. Although Blair favors the euro, Britons have been very resistant about giving up the pound as their standard currency.

Blair was also busy with domestic matters, instituting the Welfare to Work program at a cost of 3.5 billion pounds. Welfare to work was created to train 250,000 unemployed young people in service work and various trades such as carpentry. There has been some controversy over the program, however, because it is nearly compulsory. An overall program for welfare reform, however, has been slow in coming. Blair, who regards a welfare system as weakening family ties and personal responsibility, has instituted reforms regarding child poverty. Higher child benefits plus incentives that make it more profitable for parents to work than collect welfare are part of Blair's overall program, which, in 1999, vowed to abolish child poverty within twenty years.

The Good Friday Accords

Blair wasted little time in making himself heard internationally after taking office. In May 1997, he opened peace talks in Northern Ireland in an effort to stop the fighting that had torn the country apart for decades.

Northern Ireland has been a continuing problem for Great Britain since it divided Ireland in 1922. Southern Ireland became the independent republic of Ireland, but Northern Ireland chose to stay within the British Empire. In the late 1960s, Roman Catholics, about one-third of the population of Northern Ireland, began to protest against growing discrimination by the Protestant majority. Violence and terrorism intensified, involving Protestants against Catholics, police and British troops, and the Irish Republican Army (IRA), which is strongly against Northern Ireland remaining in the British Empire. Between 1969 and 1994, more than three thousand people were killed. During that time, Great Britain and Ireland often tried to intervene. In 1994, the IRA said it would stop the violence, but it resumed its terrorist activities in 1996. After a cease-fire agreement was reached in July 1997, peace talks began again in September.

Blair became involved and even got Conservatives on his side in the effort. On Good Friday, April 10, 1998, Blair was able to bring about a peace agreement that was endorsed by both Northern Ireland and Ireland. The agreement provided for restoration of home rule and an elected assembly with safeguards for minority rights. Both Great Britain and Ireland agreed to give up constitutional claims on Northern Ireland. One day in late May, Blair and the shadow prime minister John Major held an informal but intense question-and-answer session with students in Belfast, Northern Ireland. With their jackets off and sleeves rolled up, Blair and Major sat among the students for an earnest discussion of ways to solve the problem. It was the first time something like that had been done in British politics.

Ruins from a car bomb in Northern Ireland. Blair has opened peace talks to try to resolve the situation.

The Good Friday agreement was approved by the voters in Northern Ireland and Ireland in May, and elections were to be held that June. However, the IRA was still not satisfied, and a splinter group set off a bomb in the town of Omagh on August 15, 1998. It killed twenty-nine people, including nine children. Blair had been vacationing in France, but he returned for a news conference with Irish prime minister Bertie Ahern.

In 1999, Blair's government transferred authority to a Northern Ireland power-sharing government. Despite Blair's efforts, true peace is not yet a reality in Northern Ireland. However, the Good Friday agreement was a major achievement during his first term as prime minister. In 2001, Blair met again with Bertie Ahern to suggest reforms that would bring an end to the violence, including restructuring the police and reducing England's presence in Northern Ireland. Historians praise Blair's negotiating skills and his personal convictions as two of the reasons for what success has been achieved.

An International Peacemaker

In early 1999, Blair demonstrated his peacemaking skills in another part of the world. Thousands of people in Kosovo, a small province in southern Serbia, were being slaughtered under the direction of Slobodan Milosevic, the president of Serbia since 1990. Milosevic had begun a process of so-called ethnic cleansing in Kosovo to remove some 1.7 million ethnic Albanian residents, and he had ignored repeated warnings by the North Atlantic Treaty Organization (NATO) to stop the killings. When fifty thousand people in Kosovo were driven from their homes in June, NATO threatened the use of force.

Blair spoke forcefully and eloquently to get NATO members to agree on air strikes against Milosevic and his military machine. Many members, including the United States, had no direct stake in the fighting in Kosovo and were reluctant to get involved, especially if it meant sending ground troops and getting caught up in a larger war. Blair disagreed and explained his views in the *Independent on Sunday* newspaper on February 14, 1999:

> Some people argue that Kosovo is a far away place that
> has little to do with Britain. Why should we get in-

Ethnic Cleansing: A New Phrase for Old Problems

The process known as ethnic cleansing, often used to describe the situation in Kosovo in which thousands of Albanians were killed or forced from their homeland in 1998, is a new name for the old problems of racism, bigotry, and hatred. The phrase means a systematic and forced removal of members of an ethnic group from a community in order to change the ethnic composition of that region. It was first used in 1992 when mass expulsions forced ethnic Muslims from their homes in eastern Bosnia-Herzegovina. In Bosnia, many of the towns that were ethnically cleansed were eventually occupied by members of another ethnic group, who in some cases had been cleansed themselves. In Kosovo, those who escaped the killings fled to camps that were set up in Macedonia and Albania. Within a short time, these thousands of refugees overflowed the camps, resulting in food shortages, malnutrition, and rampant health problems. Those who escaped the killings but did not flee were forced into hiding from government troops. When they were eventually discovered or had to surrender because of starvation, they often suffered mass executions.

volved? Why there? To them I say I will not ignore war and instability in Europe. Fighting in Bosnia since 1991 has shown we cannot take our continent for granted. Our responsibilities do not end at the English Channel. If we can prevent war, we should strive to do so. More than 200,000 were killed in Bosnia and some 2 million forced from their homes. Fleeing ethnic cleansing and destruction in their own lands, many have ended up as refugees right across Europe, including in Britain. We do not want that repeated in Kosovo, but it could be.[44]

NATO launched an air offensive against Serbia in March 1999. The day before the strike, Blair said, "Justice is all that those poor people, driven from their homes in their thousands in Kosovo, are asking for, the chance to live free from fear. We have in our power the means to help them secure justice and we have a duty to see that justice is now done."[45]

Serbia retaliated against the air war by terrorizing the people of Kosovo. Thousands were forced to flee. In June, a multinational force entered Kosovo to restore peace, and most of the refugees had returned by September.

Blair was hailed both at home and abroad for his forceful leadership in promoting the air strikes against Serbia. Said the *Sun,* "With true moral courage, Blair has seized control of NATO and made himself a giant of the free world."[46]

The Second Election

As Labour neared its first election after taking power, Blair could point to his accomplishments both at home and abroad with justifiable pride. Inflation, interest rates, and unemployment were all the lowest the country had seen in twenty-five years. Income for the average citizen was rising. The crime rate was falling in the streets.

Those statistics were good, but Blair knew that the British public was still very troubled about some problems, especially the health care, education, and transportation systems throughout the country. He tried to indicate his awareness of their dissatisfaction by stressing over and over during the campaign that "We have a long, long way to go."[47]

Despite a low voter turnout of less than 60 percent, Blair and Labour did win a second term in June 2001. It had been many years since a Labour government was rewarded with a second consecutive term in office. Blair won with 40.8 percent of the vote, not overwhelming but enough to secure more than one-third of the seats in Parliament.

War on Terrorism

Three months into his second term, Blair stood up as America's staunchest ally when the United States was attacked by terrorists on September 11, 2001. Soon after the attack, Tony Blair flew to the United States to declare Britain's support. He stood with U.S. president George W. Bush, pledging Britain's military aid as well as emotional support. Since that time, Blair has given stirring speeches and jetted from country to country to rally the world against terrorism. He speaks passionately of a grand-scale fight against terrorism worldwide. He wants to unite countries to help bring about peace between Israelis and Palestinians in the Middle East. And he wants to rebuild Afghanistan, a country that has been devastated by years of harsh, repressive government and is

New York's World Trade Center under terrorist attack on September 11, 2001.

the scene of fighting today as the United States and its allies try to root out terrorists believed to be hiding there. "Some say this [intention to fix these things] is utopian," said Blair, "but the point I am making is simply that self-interest for a nation and the interests of the broader community are no longer in conflict. In the war against terrorism the moralists and the realists are partners."[48]

Trouble at Home

In Britain, Blair has found it to be more difficult than he expected to deliver on promises to reform the government. Shortly after he took office, he promised improvements to British schools, railroads, and hospitals. These have been slow in coming. The British people for the most part are pleased with what Blair has promised, but they appear to be growing impatient with the slow results. The government is getting a reputation for talking about problems rather than fixing them.

Blair meets with former New York City mayor Giuliani. Blair strongly supports the United States in the fight against terrorism.

An article in the *Economist* in February 2002 spoke of the prime minister's reputation:

> Mr Blair has always had something of a sincerity gap. His saintly, "I'm a straight kinda guy," pose will not have fooled many voters. He and his government have consistently overpromised, both in grandiose speeches and in spin-doctors' claims, that every modest, incremental reform is the most radical change since 1945. But in politics, trust is relative. Voters expect politicians to exaggerate, and even to be a bit devious. Mr Blair's advantage has been that he and his team looked more trustworthy––and certainly more credible—than the main alternative, the conservatives. It is that relative advantage that he is now in danger of destroying.[49]

One major and continuing domestic problem for Blair is the British educational system. This was pointed out in a *Time* magazine article discussing the needed improvements in British schools, which declared, "One adult in five can't read well enough to find a plumber in the Yellow Pages."[50] Before he became prime minister, Blair spoke often of the problems in British education and how dedicated he is to fixing them. In a 1996 speech at a Labour conference, he said, "Ask me my three main priorities for government, and I tell you: education, education, education."[51] But once in office, very little happened. Blair had to wait for two years until education money became available because of the Conservative spending plans that were in place. One of Blair's first moves was to point out by name the British schools that were failing. Instead of shaming the schools into doing better as was intended, the printed list caused middle-class students to run from the now openly failing schools, and teacher morale sunk to a new low.

However, Labour under Blair has instituted reforms. In all state primary schools, a certain number of hours are now devoted specifically to reading, writing, and arithmetic. New testing plans, introduced by the Conservatives, have been intensified. Admittedly, changes in education take time to show pro-gress, and Blair does seem committed to making real changes in a system that has long been on the decline. In fact, in a speech to an audience mostly of teachers, before baby Leo was born, Blair said, "I think I would be the first British Prime Minister that there's been that has sent all my children through the state education system."[52]

Transportation and Health Care

Blair has another huge domestic problem in dealing with England's crumbling transportation system, which has suffered from years of neglect. New trains are needed and hundreds of miles of tracks must be replaced. Great Britain's highways are also in dreadful shape. They need repaving and rebuilding. Although the Labour government has poured money into the rail system, these changes are slow in coming as well. The contrast between the English and the French progress in transportation over the years is obvious for passengers taking the 185-mile-per-hour

As prime minister, Blair has had to deal with transportation issues, such as fixing the dilapidated rails of the British section of the Eurostar Train tracks.

train from Paris to London. After the speedy, smooth ride from France, the train gets through the tunnel beneath the English Channel and then barely stutters to its destination. Officials say it will cost millions just to repair the cracked rails.

Perhaps an even more expensive problem for the government in power to fix is England's tottering National Health Service. For years, there have been complaints that this medical service, which is supposed to take care of all health needs, has been suffering from inefficiency, operations that are often canceled, and absurdly long waits for treatment. Under Blair, Labour has poured billions of pounds into improvements. Yet Great Britain still spends a smaller share of its national budget on health than does any other industrialized nation in the world. As a result, a patient who needs a hip operation might have to wait six years. It might take as long as two years to get an appointment with a psychologist. An example of the tragedy that an appointment delay can cause is that of Mavis Skeet. She needed an operation for throat cancer, but the operation was postponed four times. The winter of 1999–2000 was particularly bad in England, and all the intensive care beds in Leeds General Infirmary were occupied by flu patients. So, Skeet had to wait her turn. But by the second week of January 2000, when a bed opened up, her cancer was declared inoperable, and she died six months later. This was exactly the sort of tragedy that caused Labour to heap tons of criticism on the Conservative government during its years in power.

The death of Mavis Skeet was an example of the fact that a change in government had not produced a significant change in the National Health Service (NHS). Blair explained that more money had indeed been allocated to the NHS but that it would take time to show results. He predicted 2003–2004 as the target date when British patients can expect more hospital beds to be available and shorter times to wait for operations or other treatment. Some experts believe that improving the NHS by that date will be nothing short of a miracle.

Continuing stories of neglect and inefficiency have not helped Blair's predictions of improvement in the NHS. For instance, the *New York Times* carried the story of Ruth Addis, a ninety-four-year-old patient who had suffered a head wound and had gone to the crowded emergency ward of Whittington Hospital in north London. Addis was discovered forty-eight hours later by her daughter. The elderly woman was still in the same chair in the same emergency room cubicle where she had been admitted. She was still wearing the same clothes, and she had not been cleaned up; her head wound was caked with blood. A reporter for the *Times* in January 2002 said of Addis, "She has become the latest high-profile example of the problems confounding Britain's creaky National Health Service."[53]

The Future

Britain likes and respects Tony Blair. The country is changing in the direction that Blair the modernizer wants it to go. But besides wanting involvement in the European Union and a greater role for Great Britain in international problems, Blair

Blair continues to press forward with great dedication and confidence in his attempts to reform and modernize Great Britain.

has not yet laid out a clear plan for the future. Some mystery still remains about this prime minister. There is little doubt that he likes his job. He is hardworking, confident, and dedicated. However, he is curiously cautious at times, and it is not yet evident that he can achieve the internal reforms that he promised for his country. Only time will tell if Tony Blair is more charisma than substance or if, indeed, a true twenty-first-century man is working behind that easy smile.

Notes

Chapter 1: From Scotland to London

1. Quoted in Jon Sopel, *Tony Blair: The Moderniser*. London: Michael Joseph, 1995, p. 8.
2. Quoted in Sopel, *Tony Blair,* p. 9.
3. Quoted in John Rentoul, *Tony Blair: Prime Minister*. New York: Warner, 2001, p. 3.
4. Quoted in Rentoul, *Tony Blair,* p. 5.
5. Quoted in "Tony Blair," in *Encylopedia of World Biography,* vol. 18. Detroit, MI: Gale, 1998, pp. 117–118.
6. Quoted in Sopel, *Tony Blair,* p. 16.
7. Quoted in Rentoul, *Tony Blair,* p. 20.
8. Quoted in Rentoul, *Tony Blair,* p. 28.
9. Quoted in Sopel, *Tony Blair,* p. 23.
10. Quoted in Rentoul, *Tony Blair,* p. 35.
11. Quoted in Rentoul, *Tony Blair,* p. 54.

Chapter 2: Changing the Old Guard

12. Quoted in "Tony Blair, Prime Minister of the United Kingdom," in *Current Leaders of Nations.* Detroit, MI: Gale, 1998.
13. Quoted in Rentoul, *Tony Blair,* p. 82.
14. Quoted in "Tony Blair, Prime Minister of the United Kingdom."
15. Julian Glover, "Tony, the Straightest Guy in Town," *New Statesman,* October 30, 2000, p. 7.
16. Quoted in Rentoul, *Tony Blair,* p. 192.
17. Quoted in Rentoul, *Tony Blair,* p. 246.

Chapter 3: The Race to the Top

18. Ivor Crewe, Brian Gosschalk, and John Bartle, *Political Communications: Why Labour Won the General Election of 1997.* London: Frank Cass, 1998, p. 6.

19. Quoted in Nicholas Jones, *Campaign 1997: How the General Election Was Won and Lost.* London: Indigo, 1997, p. 16.
20. Quoted in Rentoul, *Tony Blair,* p. 310.
21. Quoted in Crewe et al., *Political Communications,* p. 140.
22. Quoted in Crewe et al., *Political Communications,* p. 135.
23. Quoted in Crewe et al., *Political Communications,* p. 141.
24. Quoted in Crewe et al., *Political Communications,* p. 139.
25. Quoted in Rentoul, *Tony Blair,* p. 300.
26. Quoted in Rentoul, *Tony Blair,* p. 575.
27. Quoted in Rentoul, *Tony Blair,* p. 316.

Chapter 4: Blair's Personal Life

28. Quoted in Mary Riddell, "Family Fortunes," *New Statesman,* April 25, 1997, p. 22.
29. Quoted in Riddell, "Family Fortunes," pp. 22–24.
30. Quoted in Riddell, "Family Fortunes," pp. 22–24.
31. Quoted in Riddell, "Family Fortunes," pp. 22–24.
32. Quoted in Patrick Rogers, "Working Woman," *People Weekly,* May 19, 1997 pp. 201–203.
33. Quoted in Rogers, "Working Woman." pp. 201–203.
34. Riddell, "Family Fortunes," pp. 22–24.
35. Quoted in Rentoul, *Tony Blair,* p. 328.
36. Quoted in ABC News.com, "Wife of Prime Minister Doing Well After Birth." http://abcnews.go.com.
37. Quoted in ABC News.com, "Wife of Prime Minister Doing Well After Birth."
38. Quoted in *Washington Post,* "The Blair Retch Project," July 7, 2000, p. CO3.
39. Quoted in Sopel, *Tony Blair,* p. 158.
40. Glover, "Tony, the Straightest Guy in Town," p. 74f.
41. Quoted in Jackie Ashley, "The Rise and Rise of President Blair," *New Statesman,* November 5, 2001, p. 10.

Chapter 5: A New Look for the New Century

42. Quoted in Rentoul, *Tony Blair,* p. 323.
43. Quoted in Rentoul, *Tony Blair,* p. 345.
44. Quoted in "Country Overview," UK online. www.fco.gov.uk.
45. Quoted in Rentoul, *Tony Blair,* p. 525.
46. Quoted in Rentoul, *Tony Blair,* p. 528.
47. Quoted in J.F.O. McAllister, "Blair's Next Move," *Time,* June 11, 2001, p. 34.

48. Quoted in J.F.O. McAllister, "Tony Blair," *Time International,* December 31, 2001, p. 92.
49. *Economist,* "A Turning Point for Tony Blair?" February 23, 2002, p. 15.
50. McAllister, "Blair's Next Move," p. 34.
51. Quoted in Rentoul, *Tony Blair,* p. 501.
52. Quoted in Rentoul, *Tony Blair,* p. 505.
53. Sarah Lyall, "94-Year-Old Becomes Case Study in British Health Care Woes," *New York Times,* January 27, 2002, p. A8.

Important Dates in the Life of Tony Blair

1953
Anthony Charles Lynton Blair is born in Edinburgh, Scotland, on May 6.

1955
The Blair family moves to Adelaide, Australia, for three years.

1961
Blair attends the Chorister School in Durham, England, for four years.

1964
Blair's father, Leo, has a massive debilitating stroke.

1966
Blair attends Fettes College in Edinburgh.

1971
Blair takes a year off from school and spends time in London managing rock bands.

1972
Blair enters St. John's College at Oxford University.

1974
Blair is confirmed in the Church of England.

1975
Blair graduates from Oxford; his mother dies; he moves to London, joins the Chelsea Labour Party, and begins a one-year bar course.

1976

Blair meets law colleague Cherie Booth; both begin work for Derry Irvine.

1980

Blair marries Cherie Booth at Oxford.

1982

Blair loses the bid for a Beaconsfield seat in the election.

1983

Blair wins a seat in Parliament for Sedgefield.

1984

Blair's son Euan is born.

1985

Blair's son Nicholas is born.

1987

Blair becomes deputy to the shadow trade and industry secretary.

1988

Blair enters the shadow cabinet as the shadow energy secretary; daughter Kathryn is born.

1989

Blair is appointed shadow employment secretary.

1992

Blair is appointed shadow home secretary.

1994

Blair is elected the leader of the Labour Party after the death of John Smith.

1995

Blair leads the fight for a new Clause IV.

1997

Blair becomes prime minister.

1998

Blair secures the Good Friday peace agreement with Northern Ireland.

1999

Blair leads fights in NATO to aid Kosovo.

2000

Son Leo is born.

2001

Blair is elected to a second term as prime minister.

For Further Reading

Books

Helen Arnold, *Great Britain.* Austin, TX: Raintree, 1996. Attractive illustrations highlight this look at Great Britain.

Daniel De Bruycker, *Scotland.* New York: Barron's, 1995. A tour through the main attractions of Blair's beautiful homeland.

Ian James, *Inside Great Britain.* New York: Watts, 1988. Good coverage of the people and places from ancient times to the present.

Michael Kronenwelter, *Northern Ireland.* Minneapolis, MN: Lerner, 1997. Covers the long and colorful history of this troubled land.

Roxie Munro, *The Inside-Outside Book of London.* New York: Dutton, 1989. An in-depth look at Britain's capital city in pictures and text.

Philip Steele, *Great Britain.* New York: Crestwood, 1994. Explores old and new Britain from Scottish castles to Buckingham Palace.

Websites

Britain's Prime Ministers (www.Britannia.com/gov/primes). The prime minister's site.

Britain USA (www.BritainUSA.com). British information service. To Downing Street (www.number-10.gov.UK). Data on the prime minister's residence.

Works Consulted

Books

Ivor Crewe, Brian Gosschalk, and John Bartle, *Political Communications: Why Labour Won the General Election of 1997.* London: Frank Cass, 1998. Discusses the role of advertising and the media in the campaign.

Current Leaders of Nations. Detroit, MI: Gale, 1998. Contains a biography of Blair that emphasizes his current status as prime minister.

Encyclopedia of World Biography. Vol. 18. Detroit, MI: Gale, 1998. Contains a short biography of Blair covering his early years to the present.

Nicholas Jones, *Campaign 1997: How the General Election Was Won and Lost.* London: Indigo, 1997. A detailed look at British election politics.

———, *Sultans of Spin.* London: Gollancz, 1999. Dissects the 1997 campaign.

Peter Osborne, *Alastair Campbell: New Labour and the Rise of the Media Class.* London: Aurum, 1999. Focuses on media's role in the 1997 British election campaign.

John Rentoul, *Tony Blair: Prime Minister.* New York: Warner, 2001. A detailed biography from Blair's childhood until his second election as prime minister.

Jon Sopel, *Tony Blair: The Moderniser.* London: Michael Joseph, 1995. A readable unauthorized biography that ends before Blair's election as prime minister.

Periodicals

Jackie Ashley, "Blair Has Stolen Everyone's Clothes," *New Statesman,* June 4, 2001.

———, "The Rise and Rise of President Blair," *New Statesman,* November 5, 2001.

Malcolm Beith and Babak Dehghanpisheh, "Keeping Everybody Happy," *Newsweek International,* June 18, 2002.

Economist, "Labour's Taliban Tendency: British Politics," November 17, 2001.

———, "A Turning Point for Tony Blair?" February 23, 2002.

Julian Glover, "Tony, the Straightest Guy in Town," *New Statesman,* October 30, 2000.

Sarah Lyall, "94-Year-Old Becomes Case Study in British Health Care Woes," *New York Times,* January 27, 2002.

J.F.O. McAllister, "Blair's Next Move," *Time,* June 11, 2001.

———, "Tony Blair," *Time International,* December 31, 2001.

Stryker McGuire, "Bush and Blair: A New Affair?" *Newsweek,* June 18, 2001.

———, "The W and Tony Show," *Newsweek International,* February 26, 2001.

Newsweek International, "Blair for the Record," December 3, 2001.

———, "Onward Christian Soldier," December 3, 2001.

Mary Riddell, "Family Fortunes," *New Statesman,* April 25, 1997.

Patrick Rogers, "Working Woman," *People Weekly,* May 19, 1997.

Martin Walker, "Blair's Britain," *Wilson Quarterly,* Autumn 2001.

Washington Post, "The Blair Retch Project," July 7, 2000.

Internet Sources

ABC News.com, "Wife of Prime Minister Doing Well After Birth." http://abcnews.go.com.

Index

Picture Credits

Cover photo: Associated Press, AP

© AFP/CORBIS, 65, 75, 80

© Sean Aidan; Eye Ubiquitous/CORBIS, 54

© Paul Almasy/CORBIS, 58

© Associated Press, AP, 33, 42, 46, 50, 53, 56, 64, 70

© Associated Press, The Nation, 13

© Associated Press, R. Pool, 68

© Corel, 18, 25

© Owen Franken/CORBIS, 78

© Jason Hawkes/CORBIS, 17

© Hulton/Archive by Getty Images, 7, 15, 27, 28, 32, 36, 39, 41, 49

© Photo B.D.V./CORBIS, 67

© Reuters New Media, Inc./CORBIS, 23, 60, 74

© Patrick Ward/CORBIS, 10

About the Authors

Corinne J. Naden, a former U.S. Navy journalist and children's book editor, has written more than seventy nonfiction books for young readers. She lives in Tarrytown, New York.

Rose Blue also has more than seventy books to her credit, both fiction and nonfiction for young readers. Her books have appeared as TV specials and have won many awards. A native New Yorker, she lives in Brooklyn.